The Rule
in Bits and Pieces

The Rule
in Bits and Pieces

EDITED BY

FR. DONALD S. RAILA, O.S.B.

Sacred Winds Press
Saint Louis
MMXIV

THE RULE IN BITS AND PIECES. Copyright © 2014 by Donald S. Raila. All rights reserved. No part of this book may be reproduced in any form or by any means without permission from the author or publisher except in the case of brief quotations for use in critical articles and reviews.

ISBN 978-1-940777-18-4

Sacred Winds Press
www.sacredwindspress.com
Saint Louis, Missouri

Nihil Obstat:
The Reverend Monsignor Larry J. Kulick, VG, JCL
Censor Liborum

Imprimatur:
The Most Reverend Lawrence E. Brandt, JCD, PhD
Bishop of Greensburg
Date: July 15, 2014

The nihil obstat and imprimatur are official declarations that a book or pamphlet is free of doctrinal or moral error. No implication is contained therein that those who have granted the nihil obstat and imprimatur agree with the contents, opinions or statements expressed.

This book is set in Minion Pro, designed by Robert Slimbach for Adobe Systems. It was inspired by the elegant and highly readable typefaces of the late Renaissance. Titles are set in Trajan Pro, designed by Carol Twombly for Adobe Systems. It is based on the *capitalis monumentalis* inscribed in the base of Trajan's Column.

Unless otherwise noted, all passages from the *Rule of St. Benedict* are taken from *RB 1980*, Copyright 1981 by Order of Saint Benedict. Published by Liturgical Press, Collegeville, Minnesota. Reprinted with permission.

I would like to dedicate this book to the Oblates of Saint Benedict affiliated with Saint Vincent Archabbey, living and deceased. Through their example of living the *Rule* and their sharing of insights about the *Rule*, many Oblates have helped me in my own understanding of the *Rule* and in my efforts to live the *Rule* as a professed monk.

Contents

Foreword   XI
Introduction   XIII

Prologue	3
Chapter 1	13
Chapter 2	15
Chapter 3	26
Chapter 4	31
Chapter 5	38
Chapter 6	42
Chapter 7	47
Chapter 8	79
Chapter 9	81
Chapter 10	83
Chapter 11	84
Chapter 12	88
Chapter 13	90
Chapter 14	93
Chapter 15	94
Chapter 16	96
Chapter 17	97
Chapter 18	100
Chapter 19	105
Chapter 20	109

Chapter 21	110
Chapter 22	112
Chapter 23	114
Chapter 24	115
Chapter 25	117
Chapter 26	118
Chapter 27	120
Chapter 28	122
Chapter 29	124
Chapter 30	125
Chapter 31	127
Chapter 32	132
Chapter 33	133
Chapter 34	135
Chapter 35	139
Chapter 36	141
Chapter 37	144
Chapter 38	146
Chapter 39	147
Chapter 40	148
Chapter 41	150
Chapter 42	151
Chapter 43	153
Chapter 44	156
Chapter 45	158
Chapter 46	160
Chapter 47	162
Chapter 48	164
Chapter 49	169
Chapter 50	171
Chapter 51	173
Chapter 52	174
Chapter 53	175

CHAPTER 54	178
CHAPTER 55	179
CHAPTER 56	180
CHAPTER 57	182
CHAPTER 58	183
CHAPTER 59	187
CHAPTER 60	188
CHAPTER 61	190
CHAPTER 62	194
CHAPTER 63	196
CHAPTER 64	200
CHAPTER 65	205
CHAPTER 66	207
CHAPTER 67	208
CHAPTER 68	209
CHAPTER 69	211
CHAPTER 70	213
CHAPTER 71	215
CHAPTER 72	216
CHAPTER 73	221

APPENDICES

RULE OF LOVE	225
CONTRIBUTOR BIOGRAPHIES	227
READING SCHEDULE	243
OTHER TITLES	247

Foreword

BY

ABBOT JEROME KODELL, O.S.B

☙

For centuries, Benedictine monks and nuns have been keeping the Holy Rule of their founder, St. Benedict, a reality in their lives by reading short sections of it in a community setting daily, usually at Midday Prayer or during a silent meal. For this practice, the Rule has been divided into 122 sections so that the complete Rule will be read in the community three times during the year.

A wonderful development growing out of the renewal of monastic life promoted by Vatican Council II (1962-95) has been the steadily growing interest of lay people in Benedictine spirituality. This interest has reached well beyond the Catholic Church and generated books of Benedictine commentary and spiritual teaching from a spectrum of Christian communities. There is an innate sense of ownership of this tradition by all Christians, since it goes back to the sixth century, long before divisions in the Church.

Another enrichment has been the revival of interest in the Benedictine Oblate movement, in which lay persons and other religious and clerics offer themselves (hence "oblate," from the Latin for "offered") in a spiritual association with a Benedictine community. Oblates live Benedictine prayer practices and spiritual values according to the reality of their own situation and environment.

Father Donald Raila, Director of Oblates at Saint Vincent Archabbey, has assembled a delightful collection of comments on the daily segments of the Rule by monks and Oblates, all practitioners of Benedictine spirituality according to their particular calling. I think all readers will find in this potluck several flavors that will suit their appetite and they will be impressed at the way the Rule can speak to various ways of life.

Introduction

❧

Some Christians have undertaken the task of simply reading the entire Bible from Genesis to Revelation over a set period of time. Some of them have attested to the value of this kind of spiritual exercise. However, such a marathon of reading, which would be difficult to pursue with ample time for prayerful reflection, may not be the best way to approach the Bible, at least not for most people. In most circumstances, it is more productive to read slowly and prayerfully and to take just a word, a phrase, a verse, or perhaps (at most) a few verses at a time. This method of *lectio divina* helps the Christian devoted to God's word to be a true listener and to enter into dialogue with God Himself.

The same principle might be applied to reading the *Rule* of Saint Benedict. It has been authoritatively said that because it was <u>written</u> in a prayerful spirit, so to speak as *lectio divina*, it should also be <u>read</u> as *lectio divina*. Thus it is best to read the *Rule* in small portions, slowly and reflectively. Many monks and Oblates have taken on the traditional custom of reading one of 122 sections of the *Rule* each day. This pre-established division of the *Rule* enables the reader to cover the whole document three times a year.

Early in 2013, one of our Oblates who follows this procedure suggested to me that it would be desirable to have a book of reflections to accompany such daily readings, especially since some of the passages are difficult to understand or to apply to modern life. She had prayerfully pondered the issue for some time before she brought it up.

xiii

THE RULE IN BITS AND PIECES

Never having heard of such an endeavor, I thought it would be worthwhile, as long as others would be assisting me. When I approached Archabbot Douglas about the matter, he was very supportive. When I mentioned the possibility to Joseph Reidhead of Sotina Publishing, he likewise expressed the desirability of such a book and thought that it indeed might result in a publishable work.

Several months later I learned, thanks to another of our Oblates, that there was already a commentary for Oblates written according the 122-part division of the *Rule*. This book, recently reprinted by WIPF & STOCK in Eugene, Oregon, was written in French by Canon G.-A. Simon, an Oblate of St. Wandrille Abbey in France, in 1934, and it was translated into English in 1946 by Leonard J. Doyle, an Oblate of St. John's Abbey in Collegeville, Minnesota. In his introduction to the book, Canon Simon mentions that "in 1925, the Right Rev. Dom Bernard Laure, Abbot of Hautecombe, brought out, especially for the Oblates, the *Règle du Patriarche Saint Benoît, Texte, Traduction, Commentaire*" (page xxii). Thus the idea of assembling a book for Oblates based on the division into 122 sections (which Canon Simon says comes from "the daily readings followed in the French Congregation" (page xxii)) is not entirely new. However, the newness of the present work lies in its not being a commentary in the strict sense of the word but a set of personal reflections. Furthermore, these reflections were composed by twenty-first century monks and Oblates and often refer to situations faced by twenty-first century people, which in many ways are different from the situations of people living in the 1930's.

It is hoped that this book will assist many Oblates (and others who are attracted to the *Rule*) to read the *Rule* more fruitfully and to gain more personal meaning from it.

INTRODUCTION

By approaching it with greater comprehension and personal insight, the reader may be led to deeper conversion as a Christian and thus also to greater ability to share his or her faith with others. In this era of "New Evangelization," may this little work help Oblates and monks to cooperate more fully with God's lavish graces in the little things that they do each day and thus to become better beacons of hope in a world immersed in much hopelessness stemming from the "culture of death."

Finally, it might be appropriate to mention here that the *Rule* of Saint Benedict is not a "rule book" (as some call it) or a "book of rules." Nor is it correct to call the chapters "Rule Number 1," "Rule Number 2," etc. (as some people tend to do). The *Rule* is a book of Christian wisdom, based largely on Scripture as well as on several centuries of monastic tradition. It is to be savored, prayed over, and lived out. Indeed, there are many regulations, but these are not generally followed literally today; many of them could not be. However, beneath the regulations and beneath all the passages of the *Rule* are underlying values which remain relevant for monks and Oblates today. The purpose of reading the *Rule* is not so much to establish rules for oneself (although in some cases that may be a praiseworthy outcome) as to encounter God, to listen to God, and to participate in His loving plan more wholeheartedly. Reading the *Rule* in short sections can help the Christian pilgrim to tap into the underlying wisdom in each section and to apply it to daily life. Pondered in "bits and pieces," the *Rule* can become a channel of "living water" (cf. Jn 4:10), of graces from Christ that open the heart to ever deeper conversion in His love.

I would like to express my gratitude to Archabbot Douglas Nowicki, O.S.B., for his support of this project; to all the monks and Oblates who have contributed reflections to this collection; to the Oblate who first made the suggestion; to Br. Joachim Morgan, O.S.B., the assistant Director of Oblates, for his indispensable help in gathering the reflections on computer; to the Oblate volunteers who have helped to proofread the text; and to Joseph Reidhead of Sotina Publishing for his readiness to publish this book and for his careful additional editing. Most of all, all thanks and praise are due to God, who makes all good things possible and who works through people and situations to encourage us to persevere in completing what He wishes us to do even when it seems impossible.

The Rule
in Bits and Pieces

PROLOGUE
1-7

"Listen carefully, my son ..."

Prologue: 1

☙

SAINT BENEDICT BEGINS the Prologue to his *Rule* with a personal admonition to listen or to pay attention to "the master's instructions, and attend to them with the ear of your heart" (Prol: 1). The Prologue is a beautiful summary of the Spirit-filled wisdom of the Bible. It asserts that ultimately it is the voice of the Lord, our teacher, who is calling to us. Saint Benedict goes beyond the necessity of paying attention in the practical affairs of life – from diagnosing an illness to driving a car. He says to his monks and to all of us: "You must listen with the ear of your heart." This means that we must pay attention to other persons with love in order to discover the truth often hidden in their life situations. Love and truth are inseparable in human life because love and truth are inseparable in God. Separated from truth, love becomes a perverted love. How often, for example, in our subjective culture of relativism, behavior following upon illusory, romantic protestations of love leads to hurtful consequences? Saint Benedict teaches us that if we wish to be disciples of Christ in a community and live in His Spirit, we must listen to one another. Only then can we respond with love which is in truth and which is life-giving.

ARCHABBOT DOUGLAS R. NOWICKI, O.S.B.

PROLOGUE
1-7

"The labor of obedience
will bring you back to him …"

Prologue: 2

☙

Here at the very beginning of his *Rule*, Saint Benedict gets to the core of the monastic life as it reflects the life of our Lord Jesus Christ; and that core is obedience. The monk must become obedient to the will of the superior of the monastery just as Christ was obedient to the will of His heavenly Father. Loving obedience to God's will is the source of our salvation, and the abbot stands in the place of Christ in the monastery.

If we return to the Latin root of the word "obedience," we see that it comes from the word meaning "to listen to intently." If we are going to obey someone, we must be able to hear what the person is asking us to do. Only when we know what he or she wants can we carry it out. Being able to hear accurately what another is saying requires the condition of silence, both the outer silence from environmental noise and the inner silence which enables us to focus on what is being said. Both types of silence are necessary, especially when we are listening to God, for He speaks distinctly but usually very quietly. The attaining of inner silence is aided by the practice of the virtue of humility, for humility removes the inner obstacles that might block our reception of God's word. In contrast, the vice of pride lures us into doing our own will in place of the Father's. Let us pray, "Lord, may Thy will be done on earth as it is in heaven. Amen."

Fr. Ronald Gatman, O.S.B.

PROLOGUE
8-13

"Let us open our eyes to the light that comes from God …"

Prologue: 9

☙❧

I would like to focus on verses 9 and 10. Approaching this excerpt from this perspective is appealing to me because these verses express the urgency that runs throughout the passage that this is something that is attainable, something realizable. While it is easy to say to oneself, "I do want to give my all to God; surely, I do want to respond to His call," it is also easy to relegate that wholehearted response to some indistinct future, with the thought that it is beyond one's grasp at the moment. This passage, which can serve to engender within us a genuine desire for a wholehearted response to God, does not allow us to make such relegation. When are we "*to arise from sleep*"? When are we "*to hear his voice*"? Verses 9 and 10 resoundingly respond, "Today! Right now!" Although God is not bound by time, *we* are, and consequently our answering of His call can *only* occur in the present, can only occur *today*.

Br. Matthew Lambert, O.S.B.

PROLOGUE
14-20

"Seeking his workman in a multitude of people, the Lord calls out to him and lifts his voice again …"

Prologue: 14

☙

IN THIS SECTION of the Prologue, Saint Benedict highlights God's desire for each of us fully to embrace the depth, the height, the length, and the breadth of His infinite love, already here on earth as well as for all eternity. We do this through the faithful living out of our baptismal call, initiated in and through Christ. Our response to His call, however, already anticipates, and in some ways is contingent upon, an initial awareness of His preferential love for us and our utter dependence on Him. We need "to see good days," "desire true and eternal life," and respond to His love, which leads us beyond ourselves and draws us onward to the beauty of infinity. This beauty is a matter of giving and receiving His love through our honest relationships with self and others.

Our capacity to listen and respond to His love occurs only when our hearts are recollected and focused as much as possible on Him, when we yearn to hear His call of love to us, when our greatest delight is responding to His delight for us. By keeping our tongues free from vicious talk, warding off deceit from our lips, and continually turning from evil and doing good, we realize the peace that only His love can give, which comes as a gift that is beyond all imagining and that already stretches forward unto eternal life.

LINDA ROCKEY

PROLOGUE
21-32

> "If we wish to dwell in the tent of this kingdom,
> we will never arrive unless we run there by
> doing good deeds."
>
> Prologue: 22

ঔ

ARE WE RUNNING by our own good deeds as fast as we can to get to heaven? If so, are we running as a community, as a family, to get to heaven? Are we concerned about those who are moving a little more slowly or struggling? Are we slowing down to help our brother or sister in Christ so that we can enter God's kingdom together? Are we willing to help carry our brother or sister to the kingdom of heaven because we do not want anyone in our community left behind? Jesus always walks with us to His kingdom, and sometimes He even carries us when we cannot take one more step. The apostles encouraged and helped many pilgrims to come to Jesus.

Perhaps this mutual encouragement in love is what Saint Benedict means by doing good deeds. Let us enter God's kingdom together as one. I encourage you to meditate on Psalm 15, which could be entitled "God's guest."

DEBORAH JOHNSTON

PROLOGUE
21-32

"... [Saint Paul] declared:
By God's grace I am what I am (1 Cor 15:10)."

Prologue: 31

☙

IN HIS LOVE the Lord shows us the way of life. Once we've been shown, it's up to us to act, react, or simply observe. Faith helps us decide which path to take. Some choose a "tried and true" path; others take "the road less traveled." Whichever path we choose, we must "run" to the Kingdom by performing virtuous works with the Gospel as our road map.

The important point is that we continue the process of making prudent adjustments on our journey, according to God's guidance. We must realize at the same time that it is the Lord's power, not our own, that brings about the changes that lead us to holiness.

Therefore, let us give glory to the Lord's name alone; let us graciously thank Him for leading us on the road of life, the way that leads to eternal life with Him.

DANA GRASHA

PROLOGUE
33-38

"... the Lord waits for us daily to translate into action, as we should, his holy teachings."

Prologue: 35

☙

IN THIS PASSAGE Saint Benedict refers to the conclusion of the Sermon on the Mount, the entirety of which (Matthew 5-7) serves as an architectural blueprint for the monk who wants to build his spiritual house on solid rock. There, Jesus sets daunting standards, and the monk might not think he has it in him to live up to all of them or, depending on the day, maybe even any of them. Our Lord basically tells us, "Go the extra mile; love your enemies; nurture prayer, fasting, and works of mercy; don't play at being a disciple, <u>be</u> a disciple." Benedict provides testimony that these aren't just words on a page; they can be translated into action. When the monk measures his witness against all this, he might fall prey to the accuser (the devil), who tells him not even to bother trying. Instead, Benedict encourages the disciple to wait no longer and to take the Lord at his word since He wants nothing more than to see him succeed on the path to life.

FR. THOMAS HART, O.S.B.

PROLOGUE
39-44

"What is not possible to us by nature, let us ask
the Lord to supply by the help of his grace."

Prologue: 41

☙

ONE CAN IMAGINE Our Lord saying, "To trust in My sacred heart, envelop your soul in the mercy which I have lavished upon you through My Body and Blood, which exists today, tomorrow, and always. Trust in My mercy and listen with the ear of your heart for an understanding of what I wish to complete within you, the furthering of charity in the place where you are."

Our Lord seems to be speaking through Saint Benedict to remind us that He has instructed us in His ways, that He wishes above all for us to love Him in one another, and that He loves us so deeply that the Word exists as a guide for us on the journey to holiness. This holiness is a matter of Christ's living more completely within us. What is not possible for us to do by nature is that which we, letting go of fear, must place into the hands of His mercy. As we grow in holiness, we mysteriously begin to realize more profoundly our limitations of both body and soul. The closer we move towards Him in this love and the more we know Him, the more He shows us how far away we are from His true perfection. Saint Benedict's frequent emphasis on humility helps us to realize just how dependent we are on grace.

Without grace we could fall victim to an evil zeal, which causes a soul in desperation and loneliness to focus so much on overcoming its limitations that it loses sight of its one true purpose, Love itself. Fear, the stark opposite of love, separates us from the peace of Christ, and that peace is required in order for us to carry out His loving will. In order for us to receive grace, we must be humbly repentant of our sins and open ourselves to Him through prayer. His mercy and grace are always available if we listen and are willing to receive.

The holy zeal toward which Our Lord is calling us is a matter of love. We must live in the Word-made-flesh, follow His commandments, and strive to love those whom we encounter in our particular vocations as if they were Christ Himself. We must learn to love the very opportunities He offers us at every moment to return His love so that He may live fully in us.

In time we come to depend on the need to love those whom Christ has placed into our care as a means to teach us who He is. We should thank the Lord for the graces He has offered us and ask Him to show us how we can extend His loving concern to those undergoing spiritual and temporal struggles. The sacred mystery of God's presence becomes more and more real, and we experience Him calling us to an ever deeper union of our souls with Him through the grace that He so abundantly provides.

ALICIA MACK

PROLOGUE
45-50

"Therefore we intend to establish
a school for the Lord's service."

Prologue: 45

☙

THIS SECTION OF the Prologue describes the monastery as a "school for the Lord's service." The notion of a school indicates that the monastery is a place where a monk learns to serve the Lord. It also implies that the monastery, or "school," is a place where Christ teaches his disciples to renounce self, to struggle against sin, and to grow in self-sacrifice and service to one another. Ultimately, life in the monastery is a matter of serving Christ Himself, which requires firm obedience and patient suffering, but which also leads to joy, not only in the life to come but also in this present life! Unhesitating obedience and suffering borne in solidarity with Christ enable our hearts to overflow "with the inexpressible delight of love" (Prol: 49).

Finally, it is through uniting our sufferings with those of Christ that we are able to share in His patience and thus grow in holiness. Padre Pio once said, "In patience you will possess your soul." It is only through the Cross that we come to share in the glory of heaven. We see a pattern. There is no Easter before Good Friday; there is no glory before the Cross.

BR. PIO ADAMONIS, O.S.B.

CHAPTER 1
1-13

"There are clearly four kinds of monks."

1:1

☙

As Saint Benedict tells us, there are clearly four kinds of monks, and there are clearly four ways of living out the Christian life. Cenobites are the first kind, and they teach us how to live in community and in family life. How do we live under the rules of the house and under the guidance of our parents and those appointed over us? Do we feel hindered, or are we able freely to cooperate with the rules? The effort to obey does not always come easily, but it is transforming.

The regulations for hermits teach us that we are not to run off simply to be alone and isolated; such an imperfect motive would not help us to grow. On the other hand, we all need some time for solitude. Do we take time to be silent and alone with God? Do we enter the combat that comes in this silence and thus strive against the devil and the temptations with which he bombards us in mind and body? Do we examine what distracts us and seek to overcome the distractions? Do we take time for self-examination in our lives? Do we rely on God, who supports and sustains us?

The sarabaites challenge us by their lack of discipline. Are we sometimes a "rule unto ourselves," or do we fall in line with the teachings of the Church, the regulations of our work place and our society, and the rules of our homes? We can enter into the *conversatio morum* of monastic life only if we are obedient. Furthermore, do we, in charity, seek to understand those with whom we disagree? If we have some authority to make or enforce rules, do we follow the rules we set down for others and serve as examples of obedience?

The gyrovagues are "loose cannons" who have not learned to be still. How about us? Amid our over-active society, can we slow down and settle down? How about our children? Have we taught them the value of silence and stillness? Have we challenged our teenagers to turn off the cell phone and to take time to be still? Have we challenged the adults in our lives through our own example of nurturing peace and stillness that reflects the life of Christ within us? What example do we set?

The *Rule* of Benedict will guide us to grow day by day in becoming the Christian persons that God has called us to be.

Br. Isaac Haywiser, O.S.B.

CHAPTER 2
1-5

"He [the abbot] is believed to hold
the place of Christ in the monastery …"

2:2

☙

CENOBITIC COMMUNITIES ELECT an abbot who teaches and directs them in imitation of Christ. One becomes a "child" of a teacher by studying and living his message. As Oblates we live the dual role of following the *Rule* as learners and then of leading others in our communities in various ways.

In the role of learning we might ask ourselves: who are our "spiritual parents," and where do we look for guidance in ongoing conversion? To what is our practice of stability given? What books, social media, groups, and activities support us in our Christian journeys as a good abbot would support his monks?

In the role of guiding others, we might ask who looks to us as an example of Christian living. We must strive to teach by example, and we must strive to embrace ongoing formation by growing in the virtues, especially as we seek to resolve life's conflicts and overcome its temptations. As Oblates we become "spiritual parents" as we transmit a heritage and a learned wisdom in the realms of family, work place, and other secular arenas.

RICHARD FITZGERALD

CHAPTER 2
6-10

"Let the abbot always remember that at the fearful judgment of God, not only his teaching but also his disciples' obedience will come under scrutiny."

2:6

"... the sheep that have rebelled against his care will be punished by the overwhelming power of death."

2:10

☙

ALL THE COMMANDS and advice in the *Holy Rule* are based on the precedent that the abbot is a spiritual master (see *RB 27*). The vow of obedience becomes distorted, and even perverse, when such is not the case and when the abbot becomes a law unto himself. As Saint Benedict is cautious to say elsewhere, "May it never happen" (cf. *RB* 64:3). This passage puts the fear of God into everyone, the master and the disciple alike. Furthermore, while much responsibility is placed on the abbot's shoulder on the Day of Judgment, the *Rule* does not leave the ordinary monk a loophole either. When he himself faces his own reckoning, he won't be able to plead a defense by saying: "Well, if I had a better abbot, he would have made me a better monk; so it's his fault, not mine." These verses constitute a summons to the abbot to an ever more intimate walk with the Lord and also a summons to the monk to place no blame on anyone except himself if he finds himself spiritually unprofitable. The truth of things as they really are will be disclosed in the future; so why not start now?

Fr. Thomas Hart, O.S.B.

CHAPTER 2
6-10

"Let the abbot always remember that ... his disciples' obedience will come under scrutiny."

2:6

☙

THE PRIMARY QUALITY of the abbot is his responsibility for his monks' progress in the virtue of obedience. The "flock" is described in these verses as "restive and disobedient" (v. 8); there is no mention of an obedient flock here, nor is there any statement that the goal of obedience in a community can actually be accomplished. Benedict only suggests that the shepherd be faithful and strive to reform sinful behavior.

Saint Benedict also makes each person responsible. If a monk rebels in spite of the abbot's sincere efforts, he becomes liable for his own punishment.

Oblates can find useful lessons in this passage. Although most of us do not live under a religious superior, an Oblate can be obedient in other ways: to a boss, to a parent, to the teachings of the Church, or even to the Director of Oblates. Opportunities for humility and service are always present.

Oblates are also reminded here that in the end each one is responsible for his or her own life. It is not so much that the goal of perfect obedience is achieved but that one perseveres and remains faithful. If we are faithful, God will give the growth in His time and His way.

DIANE ZELENAK

CHAPTER 2
11-15

> "… he [the abbot] must point out to them all that is good and holy more by example than by words …"
>
> 2:12

☙

THERE ARE MANY pearls hidden in this section for application to everyday life, and these are related to other sections of the *Rule* in which Saint Benedict uses pertinent Biblical quotes. The first that comes to mind is the first verse of Chapter 7, which asserts, "Brothers, divine Scripture calls to us saying: *Whoever exalts himself shall be humbled, and whoever humbles himself shall be exalted* (Luke 14:11, 18:14)." Verse 10 of Chapter 7 states, "The first step of humility, then, is that a man keeps the *fear of God* always *before his eyes* (Ps 36:2) and never forgets it." Thus whether we are an abbot, a parent, a guardian, a manager, a group leader, a dean, or a teacher, we lead by example as well as with words, ideally with the fear of God in our hearts. We need to remember that our "actions everywhere are in God's sight and are reported by angels at every hour" (*RB* 7:13).

The last part of this passage from Chapter 2 is related also to the ninth step of humility concerning silence: "for Scripture warns, *In a flood of words you will not avoid sinning* (Prov 10:19)" (*RB* 7:57). Thus a leader must not be over-critical but rather weigh his words carefully so as not to offend deliberately. Rulers must rather lead with compassion and genuine care for those in their charge. We shall in the end be accountable for all the words we utter. We should be especially vigilant about words of a judgmental nature, which may mask a tendency to overlook our own faults. Obedience must also be considered here. We must first of all be obedient to the will of God, but we must also obey others in their need or when they provide good example, even if they are officially "under" our authority. Thus the *Holy Rule* reinforces God's laws and key Biblical themes in a way applicable to monks and Oblates alike.

Thomas Trotter

CHAPTER 2
16-22

"The abbot should avoid all favoritism in the monastery."

2:16

☙

"WE ARE ALL one in Christ" (from 2:20). These words of the *Rule* echo for us today the doctrine of the Body of Christ, which is so truthfully and beautifully presented in the First Letter of Saint Paul to the Corinthians. In the Body of Christ there is not a single member who is unimportant. Likewise, within the "small church" which is the monastery, Saint Benedict reminds us that there should be no distinction made or preference given to one member over another. All members are important and necessary. The same is true of all human communities, including the family.

Saint Benedict presents us with a clear distinction, however, based not on the qualities and potential gifts of individuals but, above all, on the action of divine grace in the life of a faithful monk. What might distinguish one monk from another in the eyes of the abbot? It is the same thing which distinguishes us before Christ: good works, obedience and humility. These three virtues are proper to those who "cherish Christ above all" – of those who follow Him and wish to imitate Him, because Christ, and only Christ, "has done all things well" (Mk 7:37); "humbled himself, becoming obedient to death" (Phil 2:8); and was "meek and humble of heart" (Mt 11:29).

FR. PAULO PANZA, O.S.B.

CHAPTER 2
23-29

> "He [the abbot] should not gloss over the sins of those who err, but cut them out while he can ..."
>
> 2:26

☙

In order better to understand this passage of the *Holy Rule*, it is important to acknowledge, first of all, its historical and cultural influences, quite different from the ones we experience today. Advances in the fields of psychology and education have shown the counterproductive and adverse effects of physical punishment used as a means of correction in the past.

Nevertheless, these verses reveal a nuance of the Benedictine wisdom and an element that is very dear to the monastic tradition: balance. In order to attain the desired balance within the community, and also for an individual, Saint Benedict wishes that the abbot be, at the same time, an affectionate father and a demanding teacher. If this principle applies to the abbot, it is also true for each individual monk; the monk must be a loving son, as well as a faithful and attentive disciple. Throughout our spiritual journey this balance will always be beneficial precisely because this is the way in which we must all relate to God. We must look to him as *Abba* (Father) as we enjoy a tender and affectionate relationship with Him, but we must also never forget that He is our Teacher and most just Lord.

Fr. Paulo Panza, O.S.B.

CHAPTER 2
30-32

> "The abbot must always remember what he is and remember what he is called …"
>
> 2:30

☙❧

WHEN I FIRST read this verse, I called to mind the Scriptural reference Luke 12:48: "Much will be required of a person entrusted with much, and still more will be demanded of the person entrusted with more." Saint Benedict must have read this passage many times and surely reflected on it. He probably interpreted Luke's emphasis on being faithful to Jesus' instructions at all times and by everyone. Verse 30 in the *Rule* refers specifically to leaders who are followers of Christ and their responsibility to the task at hand. Heavy though the demand may be, the leader is to respond by preferring Christ's love to everything else and by trusting in Him as He trusted in the Father. In this way the leader lives more and more in Our Lord's service and teaches others to do the same.

> "He must know what a difficult and demanding burden he has undertaken …" (2:31)

Verse 31 is connected with obedience and humility. The leader is to persevere in faith to lead the flock entrusted to him and serve them in obedience to their individual spiritual needs. He is to set a Christ-like example so as to lead his people to ultimate salvation. He must humbly face the difficulties and burdens of his ministry, with the realization that only God's grace will enable him to serve his people with reverence for Christ in them and with sacrificial love.

"He must so accommodate and adapt himself..." (2:32)

In 1 Peter 5:5 Scripture tells us, "God opposes the proud but bestows favor on the humble." Was this not a promise and a reminder that may have guided Saint Benedict in writing the *Rule*? It reminds the abbot to stay in touch with the flock and to remain accessible. I know some beloved priests, religious, and a bishop who genuinely "walk the walk and talk the talk." They are like the inspired spiritual leaders mentioned in the *Rule*. One might refer also to Pope Francis' statement on World Youth Day in July, 2013: "The Shepherd must smell like sheep so that they will know him."

One might say of all these verses, "It is all about love in the end, all about love," as was said, in a play, by an actor playing a priest hearing the confession of a young woman.

CHERYL LAROSE

CHAPTER 2
33-40

" ... he should keep in mind that he has undertaken the care of souls ..."

2:34

☙

THERE IS AN annual media event concerning "The Ten Most Livable Cities in the U.S." One would never guess from the media hype and computer analyses that what makes a place "livable" depends mainly on personal circumstances and the quality of one's relationships with other people and with God.

The abbot in the *Rule* of St. Benedict is no stranger to practical concerns that help to make the monastery livable. He manages a local economy that includes, among other elements, buildings, a water supply, a mill, gardens, tools, kitchens, food preparation, a library, and clothing. This practical dimension of the *Rule* contributed to its becoming the dominant monastic rule in the Catholic Church. At times, however, Benedict is almost flippant in dismissing material concerns in comparison to the primacy of the "care of souls" (v. 34). In saying that the abbot should not "show too great a concern for the fleeting and temporal things of this world" (v. 33), Benedict gives advice that is as relevant to us as it was to abbots of his day. Amid the constant press of practical matters which have to be taken very seriously, we are called to remain focused on the paramount importance of caring for other people and maintaining our relationship with God.

FR. NATHAN MUNSCH, O.S.B.

CHAPTER 3
1-6

> "... the abbot shall call the whole community together and himself explain what the business is ..."
>
> *3:1*

☙

THE MONASTERY IS not a democracy. Neither, for that matter, is the Church. Some people object to this situation. Over the years many churches have developed a "congregational," or democratic, government. Many people have left organized religion to avoid being told what to believe. This exodus is a sad result of a failure to understand godly leadership.

This passage is a beautiful reflection on both godly leadership and godly discipleship. A godly leader, be he a pope, an abbot, a priest, a head of state, or a head of a household, takes into consideration the opinions of those in his charge. He is to make an effort to consult those whom the decision will affect, whenever possible, whether in a monastery, a church congregation, or a home.

Verses 1 and 2 are brilliant! The abbot "himself explain[s] what the business is." Then he ponders the disciples' response "and chooses what he judges the wiser course." A godly leader truly listens. He ponders and weighs the opinions of his followers. He doesn't just give them room to vent and then push on with his own agenda.

Likewise, godly followers don't just insist they are right. They humbly submit ideas and opinions and then pray that God will guide the appointed leader.

Let us, then, if we are leaders, consider how well we hear the voices of those whom we lead, and, if we are followers, consider how well we humbly submit our opinions to our leaders and then pray for them.

Darran Chick

CHAPTER 3
1-6

"... the Lord often reveals what is better to the younger."

3:3

☙

As the people of God head more deeply into the twenty-first century, Saint Benedict's *Rule* continues to provide timeless guidance for handling the world's ever-increasing complexity. Each day shore lines and cultural lines are blurred and brought closer together by the swelling influence of technology. Information is flowing more quickly and in greater quantity than ever before. This instant access to massive stores of information undoubtedly embodies great good for society. However, it also poses a danger if we put more trust in information itself rather than in God and in people.

In the past, information traveled much more slowly and in smaller measure; this situation fostered a need for people to seek guidance from others around them and to invest more time in deliberating before making decisions. Today, however, seeking counsel and delaying a decision can be viewed as signs of weakness. People tend to think that we no longer need much counsel since we have all the needed information on demand. From both a practical and a Christian perspective, nothing could be further from the truth. Seeking counsel as a regular discipline allows us to put in check our self-importance and self-will and to have greater assurance that we are deciding on the best course of action.

As we are taught in Proverbs 15:22, "without consultation plans are frustrated, but with many counselors they succeed."

Our holy father Benedict inculcates that teaching in us in *RB* 3 as he cautions us against making decisions without counsel. Through other people, including our younger brothers and sisters in Christ, the Holy Spirit will speak to us and illuminate for us what God wills us to do.

Jeffrey Fountaine

CHAPTER 3
7-13

> "Moreover, the abbot himself must fear God and keep the rule in everything he does …"
>
> *3:11*

☙

THE WORD ITSELF is not found in the text, but this passage is about OBEDIENCE. The phrase "no one is to follow his own heart's desire" (v. 8) leaps from the text. Perhaps it leaps out especially for those of us living in the twenty-first century, whose generation seems to believe absolutely, "It's all about me"; "I'm special"; "Can't you just make an exception for me?" In Christian life, however, everything is <u>not</u> negotiable, and common norms are essential. "[I]n every instance, <u>all</u> are to follow the teaching of the rule, and no one shall rashly deviate from it" (v. 7). This precept applies even to the abbot, and particular note is made, even to the point of admonition, for the abbot to "fear God and keep the rule" (v. 11). How much more so should I, a humble Oblate, temper my ego for the sake of the well-being of our community and the Church?

REV. JOEL HUMMEL

CHAPTER 4
1-21

"First of all, *love the Lord God with your whole heart* …"

4:1

☙

EVERYTHING PRESENTED IN the instruments of good works is dependent upon and grounded in the first "tool." This precept of love for God is the response given by Christ when He was asked what was the first and greatest commandment in the Jewish law. In essence, all good works flow from our love of God. It is that love which motivates us to carry out the second greatest commandment, which is to love our neighbor as ourselves. The second is impossible to achieve without adherence to the first, for it is the grace of God alone which makes it possible to bring about any good work. The other good works in this series, such as not to kill or steal or covet, are just the specific ways that God has shown us since the time of Moses in which we can make our love of neighbor concrete.

This first group of instruments constitutes a mixture of do's and don'ts, with a sprinkling of some corporal and spiritual works of mercy added on. Thus the instruments of good works are oriented toward taking care of the whole person: body, mind, and soul. Saint Benedict cares about the whole person and knows that when all dimensions of the person are healthy and in harmony with one another, they produce the good soil for holiness that God demands of each of us. God tells us in Leviticus: "You are to be holy, for I, the Lord your God, am holy" (cf. Lev 11:44).

FR. RONALD GATMAN, O.S.B.

CHAPTER 4
22-43

"Place your hope in God alone."

4:41

❦

IN THIS SECTION of instruments of good works, we find warnings against the vices of sloth, pride, anger, and gluttony. A vice is a habit of acting which is "excessive or out of control" (from *Christian Morality and You* by Ronald J. Wilkins). A vice is a natural dimension of humans that is carried to extremes. For example, eating is normal and natural, but it becomes gluttony when done to excess. Saint Benedict's cure for vices is to nurture moderation in all things, which is simply the virtue of temperance.

This list of tools also shows Benedict's great concern over the proper use of our tongues, and he is very right to have such concern. Saint James tells us that the tongue is a little instrument that can cause much destruction and that its wild behavior is almost impossible to curb. Still, we must make the effort. Benedict tells us not to swear, not to speak ill of those who speak ill of us, not to murmur, and not to be a detractor. At the end of this list of negative precepts, Benedict slips in, as it were, the advice "to put one's hope in God" (4:41; Leonard J. Doyle trans.). There is certainly a connection here. Our disordered speech often betrays a deep insecurity in ourselves, and to compensate we go on the offensive to speak negatively about others and thus to make ourselves feel better (at least for a brief moment!). On the other hand, if we welcome the grace to let God increase our trust in Him, we shall become more confident in ourselves;

we begin to know that He will keep us genuinely safe and secure. When we come to know our true worth and dignity in God's eyes, our "need" to put others down decreases, and we come to accept ourselves and to live in peace as God's beloved children.

Fr. Ronald Gatman, O.S.B.

CHAPTER 4
44-61

"Day by day remind yourself that you are going to die."

4:47

☙

D<small>AY BY DAY</small> my spouse reminds me that <u>he</u> is going to die. Though I am aware of this fact, I do not enjoy pondering it. This truth muddies the waters of my life. I'm supposed to contemplate my own readiness for Judgment Day, but I just get sad and miffed at my spouse for bringing up death so often. Judgment Day is not something to which I look forward since I am very aware of the heartaches I've caused Our Lord. I don't like thinking about that either. The blessing that comes out of all of this is that I pray and hope for His mercy.

"Guard your lips from harmful or deceptive speech" (4:51).

Saint Benedict's admonition is so practical and so appropriate. Gossip abounds – and destroys. Pope Francis has enjoined us to stop flailing one another with gossip. Gossip robs a person of his good name, whether it is deserved or not, the good name to which he has a right and which he needs in order to function in society. How wonderful life would be if we <u>never let anything</u> come out of our mouths that was not a blessing! Restraint in speech is an item in my daily examen.

"Do not gratify the promptings of the flesh; hate the urgings of self-will" (4: 59-60).

Now there's a daily battle! If I am to "prefer Christ above all," that "all" includes everything I might want to put into my mouth and everything that comes out of it. This is no small task. We must trust that the Lord Jesus tells us, as He did St. Paul, "My grace is sufficient for you" (2 Cor 12:9).

CHRISTINE ROSSMILLER

CHAPTER 4
44-61

"Guard your lips from harmful or deceptive speech."

4:51

☙

UPON AWAKENING FROM sleep, our thought process may begin with "Ah, I slept well," or "Is that a new ache?" or "Thank you, Lord, for a new day," or "I really need a cup of coffee."

Thoughts lie behind the way we begin our day, behind our attitudes, and behind our speech. Each new day <u>can</u> begin with the vigilance that Saint Benedict mentions in *RB* 4:51. How is one to heed this admonition? Discern your thoughts. Consider what effects your words will have: good or evil, happiness or sadness? The gift of speech is a powerful gift and tool. When our thoughts are judgmental, our speech is likely to reflect those uncharitable thoughts. When someone is made the butt of a joke, even without malice, the person may be struck down with sadness or embarrassment or may even lose hope. On the other hand, if our speech arises from a heart of love and thoughts of love, then our speech will defend the oppressed and give praise to our brothers and sisters, and joy and comfort will follow. When we guard our thoughts and our lips and thus allow only good words to leave our mouths, we contribute to the holy joy that brings about happiness and hope.

DEBRA ANN FEMIA

CHAPTER 4
62-78

"Do not aspire to be called holy before you really are ..."

4:62

☙

THE *RULE* OF Saint Benedict is truly a universal call to holiness, and this selection is a great example of why. Every line, with the exception of the final sentence, is applicable to anyone who wishes to live a holy, just, merciful and peaceable life.

Benedict begins with the point – probably especially apt for members of a monastic community – that our goal should not be to be perceived as holy, but to live a holy life in imitation of Christ. In His commandments God has given us a guidebook for growing in holiness, and to those Benedict adds several others, which focus largely on relationships with others and which are designed to foster love, patience, humility and peace.

Benedict reminds his brother monks that this journey to holiness is work; these are tools to be used in the workshop of the monastery as the monks labor, singly and together, toward their goal of union with God. Benedict reminds us all that we are in need of, and have unlimited access to, God's unfailing mercy. Through our observance of his "little rule" and with God's mercy, we will one day be united with God and then experience a joy beyond our imagining.

SUZANNE ENGLISH

CHAPTER 5
1-13

> "... they are eager to take the narrow road of which the Lord says: *Narrow is the road that leads to life* (Matt. 7:14)."
>
> *5:11*

༄

WHAT DOES THIS passage teach me? First, it teaches me to sacrifice my personal desires in favor of the direction that God shows me through different means or signs in my life. That is, I must do what humility and love for others tell me to do, even if I have to put aside my personal needs; I must not judge the circumstances in a self-centered way; God alone is the judge.

Obedience increases our personal holiness. It also makes our willpower much stronger. Each time we do something that is right but not pleasant for us at the moment, the overcoming of our inner resistance makes our willpower stronger and stronger. Then, when the time comes to act against the devil, we shall be ready for it. Without trained willpower we cannot protect holiness in our lives and in the lives of others who need our advice and help.

Next, willingly following righteousness moves us closer to God. Such choices form our souls in the directions God wants of us. The blood and flesh of our Lord Jesus Christ becomes more and more our own blood and flesh, and we move closer and closer to Him and His ideas and principles. We gain benefits in terms of eternity; we are getting more and more ready to obey whatever God will tell us on the next level of our existence. If we use this training while here on earth, it will benefit us significantly later on.

The practice of obedience helps to develop many other important virtues: humility, love for others, self-sacrifice, strong willpower (to further God's will), confidence, and resolution against the temptations of the devil. We gradually conquer our pride and orient all our efforts in the direction of God's will. God watches us every second, and if He wants us to move in different directions, He will change circumstances in our lives accordingly. We cannot lose anything by obedience, but can gain much by it.

Andrei Sergueev

CHAPTER 5
14-19

"For the obedience shown to superiors is given to God …"

5:15

❧

WHEN AT THE age of fifty I decided that the good Lord was calling me to join the monastery, I looked forward to belonging to a group of men living in community under an abbot and according to the *Rule* of Benedict. It was during the years before I professed solemn vows that the Holy Spirit helped me to have a full realization of and appreciation for obedience, especially to the abbot and to other superiors, who are his delegates. I recall that once, when I was having difficulties in responding positively to a particular change of assignment, I then wrote to the abbot, "I gave you the gift of my will; I turned my will over to yours, empowered by the Holy Spirit." People often ask me what is the central characteristic of living in the monastery. My firm answer is, "Honest and authentic obedience."

FR. WILLIAM A. BEAVER, O.S.B.

CHAPTER 5
14-19

"For the obedience shown to superiors is given to God …"

5:15

༄

OBEDIENCE IS A wholehearted action of the soul. It is the complete giving of one's will to conform to a proven set of truths set before us by Christ Jesus. We listen to our superiors in faith as we would listen to Christ. With a pure heart, we must follow the Shepherd of souls and those placed in authority over us by Him. We have choices to make to conform ourselves to His will. This submission is often not an easy matter, but it is the only way to do the will of almighty God and to find ultimate joy. Being in the world but not of it takes discipline but brings about inner peace and, in the Holy Spirit, oneness with God and with our fellow human beings.

MARGARET PERHATS

CHAPTER 6
1-8

" ... there are times when good words are to be left unsaid out of esteem for silence."

6:2

☙

IN THIS CHAPTER Saint Benedict makes it clear just how important it is for a person to watch what he or she says. Benedict is concerned about the detrimental effects that negative speech can have on the community and even cautions against too much *good* speech. He states, "Therefore, since the spirit of silence is so important, permission to speak should rarely be granted even to perfect disciples" (v. 3, Leonard J. Doyle trans.). Benedict is thus pointing to the main goal of monastic life - the acquisition of a deeper relationship with God. This goal is reflected in the very first word of the Prologue: "listen."

Listen intently as we might, if there is too much interference from verbiage, it will be difficult to hear what God is saying. This verbiage comes both from outside ourselves and from within. Recall that, in a story about the prophet Elijah, the presence of God was detected in a small, whispering breeze as opposed to a display of overwhelming power (cf. 1 Kgs 19:11-13). Elijah could never have detected God or heard His voice if there had not been a time of silence. In any communication a sender and a receiver are both required. When we are dealing with God, He is the more important sender. Our task is to hear what He is saying so that we might carry out His will for us. Often, however, it is the other way around. If we continually ask things of God, we can become incapable of hearing what He wants of us. We would do well to imitate those in Scripture who say, "Speak, Lord, your servant is listening" (the boy Samuel in 1 Sm 3: 9-10) and "Master, to whom shall we go? You have the words of everlasting life" (Saint Peter in Jn 6: 68).

Fr. Ronald Gatman, O.S.B.

CHAPTER 6
1-8

"In a flood of words you will not avoid sin (Prov 10:19) ..."

6:4

☙

IF I WERE to keep a daily log of "silence reminders," it might look like this: Minimizing radio and TV usage and other controllable external noise?—usually. Keeping most *verbal* conversations brief along with being mindful of potential temptations to pride?—working on it. Limiting Facebook time and e-mail communications?—not so well.

Often the noisiest aspect of my day is found not so much in my external environment (and I have two children), but within the heavy traffic of electronic media. Not much of a phone person and an introvert by nature, I slip easily into the convenient world of e-mail exchanges and Facebook updates. Yet cyberspace can hardly be likened to a quiet book nook. (Since beginning this reflection, I have responded twice to the siren song of the "new message alert" in e-mail.) The temptation to distract myself excessively with electronic media is ever present, especially when I am seeking to evade routine tasks. The result is that I often say too much while visiting others in cyberspace and thus lose my recollection. I dare not count how often I have damaged my interior peace by my impulsive and unedifying communications!

When meditating on *RB* 6, I am always drawn to the title word "restraint," a deliberate holding back. Perhaps I can keep my electronic devices in inconvenient places, or resolve to check messages a set number of times per day.

I might try invoking the Holy Spirit's help before communicating. Finally, I should pause before clicking "send" or "post" to prevent having later to mop up a harmful *"flood of words"* (*RB* 6:4).

Pauline Lanciotti

CHAPTER 6
1-8

" … the disciple is to be silent and listen."

6:6

☙

THIS CHAPTER IS not so much about silence as it is about the internal disposition for silence. This reality is indicated by two things. First, the Latin title does not say "silence," but "taciturnity," namely the habit of silence. Secondly, in both verse 1 and verse 3, restraint even from good speech is recommended out of respect for the habit of silence. Simple talkativeness by itself already misses an important piece of spiritual wisdom, namely that the devout disciple, instead of itching to communicate, should be intent on listening. This disposition becomes especially crucial in the life of prayer, in which the important thing is not to try to inform God about anything, but to wait for His messages in perfect silence. To say, "Speak, Lord, your servant is listening" (1 Sm 3: 9) is both a humble petition and an effective way of entering into the presence of God.

FR. SEBASTIAN SAMAY, O.S.B.

CHAPTER 7
1-9

"… we descend by exaltation and ascend by humility."

7:7

☙

ONE OF THE most important tools that a Benedictine Oblate has for his or her growth and understanding of a life lived in the service of God and neighbor is the *Rule* of Saint Benedict. Although many chapters give excellent advice regarding the everyday life of monks, one of the most profound and in-depth chapters, Chapter 7 on humility, touches all of us. Throughout human history, the gift and virtue of humility has been a subject of controversy since it can run contrary to the typical human tendencies of pride and arrogance.

Especially in today's world, where these negative traits are put forth to be highly sought-after and rewarded, humbleness regarding ourselves as we interact with others is looked upon as a weakness. Not so, according to Saint Benedict!

With many pertinent references to Scripture, Saint Benedict shows us that this humility is a beautiful trait of the gentle seekers of God. These followers' eyes are on the heaven that He has promised to those who love him and who love their neighbors as themselves. Even in the Old Testament, the psalmist prays, "LORD, my heart is not proud; nor are my eyes haughty. I do not busy myself with great matters, with things too sublime for me." (Ps 131:1). This is truly the wisdom of the God who loves us infinitely and who has given Himself to us in His Word.

Benedict goes on to present us with Jacob dreaming of the ladder of the descending and ascending angels (Gen 28:12).

Most of us are familiar with this scene, but how much more exciting it becomes when we reflect on Benedict's explanation of his "steps of humility," twelve in all, helping us to ascend the sides of this ladder (vv. 6-9).

How profoundly beautiful it is to strive for the humility to which God calls us, knowing that His love will lead us to his everlasting kingdom!

Donna Ciarcinski

CHAPTER 7
1-9

"... we descend by exaltation and ascend by humility."

7:7

☙

To reach the highest place is being willing to take the lowest place. This Gospel norm goes against common sense, and yet it is one of the keys to the kingdom Jesus has given us. It is the shortest route, the "little way." It is the way that monks, Oblates, or anyone can realize, from the heart, what the Gospel is all about and what the kingdom is like.

This precept shows how the kingdom of God turns everything upside down. The deepest wisdom is the humility to know that I am totally dependent upon God, and that He loves me as if I were the only person in the world.

To realize this makes me feel absolutely dependent upon Him. I want nothing more than to wait for Him in the lowest place. Waiting there, I experience the heavenly exaltation of knowing how much He loves me.

Once I accept this truth, my striving to exalt myself seems so foolish, so unnecessary. I have been trying to scramble up to the highest point of my abilities, of my capabilities, of my potential. I have wanted everyone to see how successful and admirable I am. I have wanted to reach a position in which I am so secure that I do not have to worry about losing my place. Then I fall down again to the bottom because I realize that someone else is higher, more successful, and more capable. I feel I have no worth. I "hit rock bottom."

Now I see that all along, while I have been scrambling higher by my own means, there has been a ladder standing right there. However, to climb this ladder, that is to ascend, I must descend, in my heart, to the lowest place that I can reach and to wait there for the Lord. Now I know what is the greatest ability the Lord has given to me: the ability to humble myself as He has humbled Himself in loving me.

Now I know that the ladder standing right there, the only ladder worth ascending, is the <u>cross</u>; for it was on the cross that the eternal Son of God showed His Father's love for the world. He showed this love by emptying Himself of His equality with God and becoming a servant, the lowest of all. What heavenly exaltation it is to share that lowest place with Him and to know His love for me!

Fr. Thomas Acklin, O.S.B.

CHAPTER 7
10-13

"He [the monk] must constantly remember everything God has commanded …"

7:11

☙

THIS FIRST STEP of humility calls us to nurture "fear of the Lord," that is, a continual mindfulness of God's presence with an attitude of reverence. Such a disposition is very much connected with the command to "pray always" (Lk 18:1) or to "pray without ceasing" (1 Thes 5:17). Remaining as connected as possible to God at every moment means thwarting temptations as soon as they come and rejoicing in blessings constantly.

Keeping such a disposition is basic not only to monastic life but to <u>all</u> Christian life, and yet it is extremely difficult for most of us. One technique that I use to remember God's presence is to keep a phrase of Scripture in my mind when I have a free interval in-between tasks, especially when I am walking down the hallway and have no one else but God in my company. More often than not, I very quickly forget the Scripture verse and start worrying about my schedule and all sorts of other trivial things. All that worry, I know, is utterly useless, and yet my regular failures show me how hard it is really to open my heart to God and put my problems into His hands! Trying to be mindful can certainly teach us humility, if only because we can be so poor at living in fear of the Lord and letting Him take charge of our minds, our desires, and our lives.

Despite our repeated failures to be recollected, we <u>must</u> keep trying! The grace of perseverance will truly be with us if we sincerely keep making renewed efforts, no matter how many times we fail. In due time God will purify our hearts and minds of useless (or perhaps even harmful) chatter until we welcome Christ to capture and transform every thought, word, and action of ours. Then some day we shall have learned to "do it [everything] in the name of Jesus" (Col 3:17) and "do all for the glory of God" (1 Cor 10:31). Then we shall be filled with the spiritual joy that Saint Benedict wants us to have (cf. *RB* 49:6, 7) and be ready for the even greater joys of heaven.

Fr. Donald Raila, O.S.B.

CHAPTER 7
14-18

> "That he may take care to avoid sinful thoughts, the virtuous brother must always say to himself: *I shall be blameless in His sight if I guard myself from my own wickedness* (Ps 17 [18]:24)."
>
> 7:18

☙

SAINT BENEDICT'S *Holy Rule* provides much detail about a monk's daily activities. Monks and Oblates are often sidetracked by a flurry of activities that compete for their attention. The culmination of one's lifelong race toward God often seems far off or at least does not seem to be a pressing concern at any given moment. The first step of humility reminds the monk intentionally to overcome laxity of thought and to remember that God constantly gazes on His people. Fear of God necessitates that the monk cultivate both mindfulness of God's presence and those habits that will lead him closer to God. Saint Benedict's choice of words and the imagery of angels reporting to God about man's deeds in verses 13-18 encourage the monk to think and act in ways favorable to his eternal well-being.

This section of the *Holy Rule* thus reminds the reader that the mind is a great battlefield where souls can be either saved or lost. Therefore, monks and Oblates must be vigilant and refrain from entertaining sinful thoughts or acts. Those who maintain custody of their thoughts and who are mindful of God's presence diminish the likelihood of forgetting about God.

Whenever we do lose mindfulness of God in our daily activities and thoughts (as we are often likely to do), let us recollect ourselves quickly and go about our day in a way pleasing to God.

JOSEPH DUCHENE

CHAPTER 7
19-23

"*They are corrupt and have become depraved in their desires* (Ps 13 [14]:1)."

7:22

☙

SAINT BENEDICT CALLS our attention to the danger of being misled by the desires of our fallen natures. Our sins were forgiven in baptism, and we are also absolved of our sins after making a good confession. However, we still have to contend with the effects of sin which result in an inclination to future sin (i.e., concupiscence). The danger of following our disordered desires has been a concern throughout history, ever since the Fall, but perhaps never more so than it is now. There are so many voices (e.g., from movies, television shows, music, advertisements) that specifically target our base desires. There is also a general denial of sin in our culture and, consequently, a denial of the effects of sin.

Saint Benedict provides the way to protect ourselves from these dangers, that is, through prayer, obedience, and humility. In the Our Father, in particular, it is helpful to focus on our petition that the Father's will be done rather than our own. We are protected through obedience by living in accord with the teaching of the Church and by obeying our legitimate superiors. Finally, we are safeguarded by recognizing our current weak, fallible state; by turning away from our selfish desires; and by humbly turning to Our Lord for continual help and guidance.

FR. NATHANAEL POLINSKI, O.S.B.

CHAPTER 7
24-30

> "... *the eyes of the Lord are watching the good and the wicked* (Prov 15:3) ..."
>
> 7:26

※

This passage can be intimidating if God is viewed as an all-seeing judge who simply watches over us to tally up our every failure. Such a view misses the truthful observations that God "is a loving father who waits for us to improve" (7:30) and who values our attention and understanding since He continually "*looks down from heaven ... to see whether any understand and seek God*" (7:27; Ps 14:2). Since we who are created in God's image authentically cherish the time and attention of those we love, it is not surprising that God our loving Father both cherishes our responses to Him and rewards those who seek Him.

The ideal motivation for seeking God and His will is the faith-filled desire to respond in love to the One who first loved us. Accordingly, Saint Benedict encourages and exhorts us to grow in love through the practices of the monastic life (see Prol: 49 and 7:68-69). However, since he also knows human nature very well, it may be that fear of God and of punishment are necessary to avoid the snares of evil and of sinful desires. In that case, such motives constitute a good first step, but it is only a first step since all that we do should ultimately be ordered to, and drawn by, the love of God.

Fr. Nathanael Polinski, O.S.B.

CHAPTER 7
31-33

> "... he [the monk] shall imitate by his actions that saying of the Lord: *I have come not to do my own will, but the will of him who sent me* (John 6:38)."
>
> *7:32*

☙☙

As I looked at the flower bed in our yard, I began to reflect on these verses, which concern God's will for us. Our hearts are like a garden; yet what is a garden? It is basically nothing more than a plot of ground until it is given care. If it is left to its own resources, the ground will become hard, and weeds will begin to sprout. The weeds at first will be few, but soon they will grow wildly out of control and overtake the whole plot until nothing harvestable will grow.

To become a garden, the ground has to be tilled and cultivated. Good seed needs to be sowed. Careful daily attention must be given to the plants, and the soil must be kept moist and soft in order to be fertile. The weeds must be pulled out before they become established and begin to spread.

Our hearts are like a garden. We need to prepare them to receive the seed of God's will by cultivating them; that is, we must make time each day to listen prayerfully for God's will. If we neglect this practice, soon our hearts will become hardened by self-will, and the weeds of selfish desires will take over. As we attend daily to the practice of spending time with God in the garden of our hearts, we come to experience the sowed seed of God's will growing in us. Amen.

Pastor Douglas Schader

CHAPTER 7
34

> "... that a man submits ... in all obedience for love of God, imitating the Lord ..."
>
> 7:34

༄

OUR LIVES AS Oblates, that is, as Benedictines in the world, are not always easy or straightforward. Just performing our daily tasks can be an occasion of great trials and, at the same time, a source of opportunities provided by God to make us holy.

Perhaps at work someone is out sick, and you are asked to change your plans by learning to perform a new task, to work overtime, or to work with a person you perceive as difficult. Are you able to accept the sudden change, or do you see it as unfair and approach the task with an "attitude"? Or maybe you've been blamed unjustly for something you didn't do and are asked to replace, repair, or redo something for which you weren't responsible. Are you still able to think of loving God in the midst of this situation and obey without murmuring or delay?

The *Rule* calls us to learn to trust God and to recognize in all hardship and adversity that He is at work and is leading us through the "narrow way" of His will. The process of such learning can help us to accept the various tasks we are given and possibly even obey *joyfully*. When we know that our loving Father is with us and that He is waiting for us to come to Him through obedience, we can receive the grace to deny ourselves and accept His will. We may even recognize that such submission brings us true freedom and the virtue of simplicity.

We are told in Scripture, "And if you obey the voice of the Lord your God, being careful to do all his commandments which I command you this day, the Lord your God will set you high above all the nations of the earth. And all these blessings shall come upon you and overtake you, if you obey the voice of the Lord your God" (Deut 28:1-2). We likewise hear, "Does the Lord so delight in holocausts and sacrifices as in obedience to the command of the Lord? Obedience is better than sacrifice, and submission than the fat of rams" (1 Sm 15:22).

Diana Martin

CHAPTER 7
34

> "... that a man submits to his superior in all obedience for the love of God ..."
>
> 7:34

☙

THE MAIN IDEA in this passage is submission to a superior. Saint Benedict uses a verse from Philippians to reinforce this thought: "He became obedient even to death (Phil 2:8)" (7:34). There is nothing to suggest that the superior is always right or always knows the best way of doing something. The aim is to become obedient to another human being out of love for God and in imitation of Christ.

When Thomas Merton entered the Trappist monastery at Gethsemani, Kentucky, he described his early experience like this: "There were no choices, there were ample penances, and Thomas Merton blossomed."

For a monk or an Oblate, obedience to another requires trust. No matter how bad or unfair something seems or what direction our life takes as a result, we can count on the Lord to help us through. Like Thomas Merton, we learn that our crosses become graces that help us grow.

DIANE ZELENAK

CHAPTER 7
35-43

"... his [the monk's] heart quietly embraces suffering and endures it without weakening or seeking escape."

7:35-36

❧

THE FOURTH STEP of humility idealizes the person whose heart quietly embraces suffering without seeking escape. Here there is a personal encounter between the heart and suffering, an embrace that is the fruit of a loving familiarity, of a longing fulfilled and a sense of homecoming. There is no sense of a frigid hug that emerges from fear and keeps suffering a safe distance away. No, this is an embrace, a total abandonment of oneself into the arms of suffering without seeking escape. A trapped animal will gnaw off one of its own limbs in order to save its own life. In contrast, the monk who has reached the fourth step of humility knows that he is not trapped, but rather freely embraces suffering with a sense of abandon, because suffering has become flesh in the obedient Christ, who freely invites the monk to gnaw upon His flesh given for him. The monk realizes that in this quiet embrace of suffering is found the heart of Christ, who left the ninety-nine sheep and found him, the straying sheep, and has endured the suffering of the cross in order that he might experience the homecoming of the prodigal son.

FR. SHAWN MATTHEW ANDERSON, O.S.B.

CHAPTER 7
44-48

> "... that a man does not conceal from his abbot any sinful thoughts entering his heart ... but rather confesses them humbly."
>
> 7:44

☙

THE CENTER OF humility is *honesty*; a simple embrace of the truth about ourselves in relation to God, who *is* Truth. In this fifth step of humility, regarding hidden faults, Saint Benedict requires honesty with our superior but also, perhaps even more importantly, with ourselves. Because of original sin we have many selfish thoughts, feelings, and behaviors which can sometimes shock us with their intensity. When we dislike what we see in the mirror, we may be tempted to hide our flaws of thought and deed even from ourselves by excusing ourselves or dismissing their reality. Yet Saint Benedict knows that the way to deal with a wound is to treat it, not ignore it. He quotes three different passages of Scripture to remind us that God's fundamental attitudes toward us are *mercy* and *acceptance*. We, not God, are the ones shocked by our sinfulness, because we have yet to accept the truth of our own weakness. We are still proud! Humbly confessing our faults carries a two-fold blessing: we are forced to make an honest assessment of ourselves, and we also open ourselves to the wisdom, counsel, and love of another. We effectively say, "I am in trouble, and I need help!" This is the reason why Saint Benedict has us confess not just to anyone but to the abbot, a person especially qualified by his position and by God's grace to assist us.

The primary way, for those of us who are Catholic, to live the fifth step of humility is through frequent recourse to the Sacrament of Reconciliation. In this way we bring our spiritual wounds to the Divine Physician before they can become infected by our neglect. In addition to sacramental confession, it is also good to have a spiritual mentor or, at least, a solid spiritual friend whom we trust and who can help keep us honest with ourselves and with God.

Br. Lawrence Machia, O.S.B.

CHAPTER 7
49-50

"... that a monk [be] content with the lowest and most menial treatment ..."

7:49

☙

THE TWELVE STEPS of humility are a journey towards "the perfect love of God which casts out fear" (7:67). This sixth step is a foundational keystone in ascending these steps. Jesus spoke of his particular love and concern for the poor and the weak. This sixth step invites us into this realm of Christ's particular love. Opening oneself to menial tasks is most certainly counter-cultural, even revolutionary, in the West. Sometimes "humiliation" precedes "humility." This typical occurrence may be why humility is so difficult for us.

However, this piece of wisdom is not just about menial work. It's also about holding the proper attitude or countenance while accepting the lesser, or even the least, place. "Insignificant and ignorant" (v. 50) is not what our culture tells us is a worthy aspiration, but relative to the privilege of continuing to live in the Presence, this radical humility is but a small price to pay.

REV. JOEL HUMMEL

CHAPTER 7
51-54

"... that a man ... admits ... that he is inferior to all and of less value ..."

7:51

༺༻

IN A SOCIETY where children are raised to believe that they are all "winners," accolades are often given for just "showing up," and some teens arrive at events in limousines; so being compared to a lowly worm is indeed a hard saying. To be told that you have to be "inferior to all and of less value" is as repugnant a concept as Jesus' telling the Jewish elders that they would have to drink His Blood to be saved.

Nonetheless, to experience full communion with God, we must deny our old ways, our old beliefs, and even our old selves. We must let go of our egos and our carefully nurtured self-esteem. If we have indeed been exalted, whether through our own diligence or through a mere sense of entitlement, we are called by the Gospel and the *Rule* to embrace a profound humility in order to become one with Christ.

The transition toward a humble disposition will surely result in spiritual confusion as we begin to examine the motivations for our actions and then see how base and prideful our motives can be. Even our good works can be rooted in pride. The remedy to this confusion is prayer, so that we may hear His voice, surrender to His will, abandon our lofty selves, and walk His path so as to become one of His flock. The opportunity to grow in humility is a great blessing.

TERESA D. WARLOW

CHAPTER 7
55

> "... that a monk does only what is endorsed by the common rule ... and the example set by his superiors."
>
> 7:55

☙

THE EIGHTH STEP of humility, addressing the monastic vice called "singularity," serves as a useful point for self-examination. Sometimes a monk, usually a novice or a junior monk, will suddenly adopt a new way of doing things, such as going barefoot. When asked about it, he invariably replies, "I think it's more monastic."

Therein he expresses a noble ideal: wanting to be more monastic. No one can fault him for that desire. After all, a monk wanting to be *less* monastic has either lost his vocation, is receiving another vocation, or is going through some kind of crisis, or maybe all three. Nevertheless, that zealous novice or junior is at fault for making a unilateral decision.

Perhaps from painful experience, Saint Benedict saw the need to prohibit such willful singularity. If one wants to live out one's own vision of monastic life or if in one's heart of hearts one wants to be something other than a Benedictine, one ought to go somewhere else and follow *that* calling. In the long run, it is counterproductive to try to be something admirable but non-Benedictine in a Benedictine monastery. As one meditates upon this seemingly severe injunction, a question worth asking oneself is whether anyone at the head table [that is, one of the superiors] is adopting such a "more monastic" practice.˙

BR. BRUNO HEISEY, O.S.B.

*   N.B.: Oblates might do well to consider the motives behind any spiritual practices that they might adopt as well as the potential fruits. Are the practices a part of the Church's tradition? Are my motives Christ-centered? Am I likely to grow closer to Christ and the Church, in love, by this practice? Or are my ego and my self-image a large part of this choice?

– Editor

CHAPTER 7
56-58

"... that a monk controls his tongue and remains silent ..."

7:56

☙

ABOUT 54 YEARS ago, when I was applying to enter the monastery at Belmont Abbey in North Carolina, the abbot in his interview with me asked the question, "What is the most important virtue practiced in the monastery?" I had read the *Rule* several times but was not really well versed in it; so after a few seconds of thought, I replied, "Humility." The abbot did not look very happy and said "No, it is charity."

Thus began a discussion between us that continued for several years. At the end of that time, I stated that one could not very well be charitable unless one was first of all humble. My reasoning then was that one had to know oneself before God with all one's particular faults and failings. This self-knowledge should then prompt one to be charitable to others who were traveling the same road to holiness in a communal lifestyle. Since we never know what burdens our brothers are bearing, we ought to vie with them in the charity that flows from the fact that we see our *own* weaknesses. We are thus able, in love, to make allowances for the weaknesses of others, the causes of which we can never fully understand. This consideration for others constitutes the good zeal that springs from humility and which leads us to anticipate one another in charity (cf. *RB* 72:4; Rom 12:10).

In dealing with silence, Saint Benedict quotes Proverbs to indicate that talking too much prevents us from realizing our true selves. Humility works hand in hand with silence since it enables us to see more clearly our reasons for speaking. Are we trying to effect an outcome that will distract others? Such a motive is prideful rather than humble. Humility often manifests itself in the practice of silence as we learn to keep our opinions to ourselves and not to try to dominate a situation or another person. People who always have something to say are not likely to be humble, nor are they fully aware of their own worth before God. Through much talking they are trying to prove themselves in the sight of others and thus yield to pride. They seem to be "filled with themselves" and their own self-importance.

On the 25th anniversary of my ordination as a priest, I received a phone call from the abbot with whom I had had the discussion more than 30 years before concerning charity and humility. I reminded him then of the discussion we had had years earlier. He then conceded that perhaps I was correct in my observation that in order to be truly charitable one had first to be humble.

When asked to name the four cardinal virtues, Saint Bernard of Clairvaux replied "humility, humility, humility, and humility." He said this because the word cardinal means "hinge," and everything hinges on humility. Humility opens the door to the hearts of others and to the heart of God. Humility is essential for us who follow a crucified Savior. What could move us more to nurture humility than the sight of Jesus hanging on the cross?

Fr. Paschal A. Morlino, O.S.B.

CHAPTER 7
59

"... *Only a fool raises his voice in laughter* (Sir 21:23)."

7:59

☙

One of my talents is the ability to help others see humor in situations and particularly in themselves. That is, I help to make people laugh at themselves. Saint Benedict is surely not against good humor and laughter since without these a monastery would be a truly gloomy place. There is nothing more dreadful than to live in a community that has no sense of humor. The *Rule,* however, reminds us that unnecessary laughter and raucous laughter are <u>not</u> good, at least in a monastery. Certain situations call for a good hearty laugh, as when things get off-kilter. Furthermore, we all need to "laugh things off" occasionally, but in such situations we need to manifest the type of laughter that is healthy and charitable. We should seek not to indulge the bad habit of breaking out into laughter at the least provocation.

We might ask ourselves what it is that brings about laughter. Laughter is a strictly human phenomenon. There is truth in the saying, "Laughter is the best cure," especially amidst a particularly sad or difficult situation. Since God has given us this special gift of laughter, it seems that God Himself must have a sense of humor. What goes against this gift is the practice of ridiculing a person or putting him down.

There is much more to the quote from Sirach than meets the eye. It seems to make room for laughter that is sincere and from the heart. An unmindful, foolish laughter might involve jeering at another person because of his or her background or lack of knowledge. Such laughter would certainly be frowned upon by the *Rule* as well as by the Gospel since it lacks all semblance of charity and reveals a failure of humility.

Time spent in silence with Jesus in the Eucharist helps us to be aware of our own place in time and space. There before the Blessed Sacrament we can better see our unworthiness, remember the merciful acts of God in our lives, and thus also welcome Him to transform the way in which we view others whom we encounter. We can learn "to see Christ in all." Letting Christ pervade our outlook on life can nurture true humility, which always seeks to lift up and affirm others. We learn to find God in the talents and even the weaknesses of others and thus come to delight in His presence in others. This kind of humility leads to meekness, which is not weakness but rather strength under control, power used to build up rather than to tear down. Genuine laughter seeks to console and build up, not to ridicule or pull down.

Fr. Paschal A. Morlino, O.S.B.

CHAPTER 7
59

"[The monk] is not given to ready laughter …"

7:59

☙

THIS VERSE ELICITS vehemently negative reactions from college students when they read the *Rule* of Saint Benedict. If there is anything that is prized highly by young people it is "laughing and chilling out." Young people learn this from their elders, for whom entertainment has become a way of life. In an age of "Saturday Night Live," we relish the art of deconstructing and laughing at anyone and anything.

Benedict's discouragement of laughter needs to be put in context. He never bans laughter entirely; rather he puts limits on it. The positive dimension of laughter he expresses with other terms such as "joy" (*gaudium*) and "delight" (*dilectio* and *delectatio*); furthermore, he dislikes "sadness" (*tristitia*) even more than needless laughter. When asked to reflect on this verse, students readily identify unwholesome types of laughter such as teasing, scorn, mockery, sarcasm, cynicism, or the avoidance of something serious. Most of us yearn to hear someone say to us, "I love you," but it is hard to take them seriously if they are laughing. God's Word to us is: "I love you, and I will be with you"; but only if we are not laughing will we be able to hear.

FR. NATHAN MUNSCH, O.S.B.

CHAPTER 7
60-61

> "... that a monk [speak] gently and without laughter, seriously and with becoming modesty, briefly and reasonably ..."
>
> 7:60

☙❧

SAINT BENEDICT CHALLENGES us to strive to reach the highest summit of humility if we desire to attain speedily that exaltation in heaven to which we climb by the humility of this present life (7:5). We are called by our Lord Jesus Christ to "be perfect as your heavenly Father is perfect" (Mt 5:48), and Saint Benedict commands us truly to seek God by preferring nothing whatever to Christ (58:7, 72:11). His twelve steps of humility guide us along this journey of holiness to union with God, beginning with the exhortation to keep the fear of God always before our eyes (7:10) and culminating in that perfect love of God which casts out fear (7:67).

In the eleventh step of humility, Saint Benedict challenges us to speak gently and without laughter. He is not interested in making his monasteries havens for somber and downcast monks! After all, he speaks in the Prologue about hearts overflowing with the inexpressible delight of love (Prol: 49). Just as Lent (which is to be a standard for the whole year) is a time to deny ourselves such things as needless talking and idle jesting in order to look forward to Easter with joy (49:7), so daily life gives us opportunities to look forward to union with God, both here and in heaven, by using the gift of speech for the glory of God and the good of others.

It is by fixing our eyes on Christ that we are best able to love God for His sake and our neighbors for the Lord's sake and for His glory. Through the proper and responsible use of language, we will guard the gift of our speech. This practice involves never drawing needless attention to ourselves or using our selfish actions or those of others as occasions to provoke laughter in conversations. This discipline will allow us, by God's grace, to reach the high summits of humility, which are essential for our journey to union with God.

Fr. John-Mary Tompkins, O.S.B.

CHAPTER 7
62-70

> "The twelfth step of humility is that a monk always manifests humility in his bearing no less than in his heart …"
>
> 7:62

☙

THE TWELFTH STEP of humility directs us to manifest humility in our bearing. We are to grasp our nothingness on account of our sinfulness and weakness. Saint Augustine admonishes us truly to "despise ourselves and wish others to treat us as we truly deserve." One should act as though he or she were always carrying about the dying of Jesus in his or her body.

Humble bearing is a matter of not expecting favors or special treatment because of our self-designated elevated status, which we may take on because of material or spiritual wealth, education, looks, age, the accomplishments of our children, or our supposed holiness. Humble bearing is wearing our gray, extra pounds, wrinkles, scars, and blemishes with a sense of self-acceptance, not reluctant resignation, denial, or shame.

Humble bearing is walking as Jesus did, as Blessed John Paul II did, and as Pope Francis does. It is being spiritually and physically approachable. It is a disposition of vulnerability, openness, gentleness, and love. Humility in bearing is not looking through, around, or beyond a person; furthermore, it is looking <u>into</u> a person with gentleness and compassion, always mercifully and never judgmentally. Humble bearing is being totally present to touch the deepest part of another person. It can be exhibited physically by something as simple as a smile, eye contact, relaxed facial muscles, and an unassuming manner that exudes a peaceful interior.

As we master the twelve steps, we dash our pride against the Cross and arrive at that perfect love of God which casts out all fear. We now burn with a divine love that lights up all that we encounter. Divine love then comes as naturally as breathing, and we can accept nothing less as an ultimate goal. We aim to love as we are loved by our Father and by Christ the Lord, for nothing more than love's sake.

KATHRYNE THOMPSON

CHAPTER 7
62-70

> "... the monk will quickly arrive at that *perfect love* of God which *casts out fear* (1 John 4:18)."
>
> 7:67

☙

Verses 67 to 70 form an epilogue to Chapter 7 as well as to the "spiritual section" (Chapters 1-7) of the *Rule*. Like the conclusion to the Prologue, the end of Chapter 4, and Chapter 73, Saint Benedict's wisdom here points us to the goal to which all the arduous spiritual practices tend: living in the "perfect love of God" (7:67) and doing everything "out of love for Christ" (7:69). This passage also implicitly reminds us of the ultimate goal of heaven since few if any of us will be fully "cleansed of vices and sins" (7:70) during our pilgrimage on earth.

Saint Paul states, "If our hopes in Christ are limited to this life only, we are the most pitiable of men" (1 Cor 15:19). Similarly, the steps of humility, as a practical way of living out the Gospel of Christ, ultimately make little sense unless we are seeking something beyond life in this "vale of tears." It might be somewhat satisfying to learn to act in virtue "as though naturally, from habit" (7:68) and "out of love for Christ, good habit and delight in virtue" (7:69); but in the end we grow weak and die, and so our only real consolation is the assurance that we are "hastening toward [our] heavenly home" (73:8).

In our very materialistic secular culture, which in the end offers us no hope, the *Rule*, like the Gospel itself, gives us the true and wonderful hope of living in perfect, loving communion with God. The *Rule* counteracts the modern trend of striving frantically for success, pleasure, popularity, and power. The *Rule* guides us through spiritual disciplines to gain glimpses of eternal glory even while we are on this earth. The *Rule* boldly asserts that the persistent practice of humility and obedience will, by God's grace, lead to a perfect joy that makes all the hard effort more than worthwhile. Let us, then, take courage as we live the "continuous Lent" (49:1) of monastic discipline since by this means God is ushering us into the marvelous place that He "has prepared for those who love him" (4:77; 1 Cor 2:9).

Fr. Donald Raila, O.S.B.

CHAPTER 8
1-4

"[The monks sleep] until a little past the middle of the night …"

8:2

☙

IN AN AGE when watches, timepieces, and electricity were unavailable, monks looked to the sun, the moon, candle power, and other elements of nature to calculate their times for praying during the various seasons. This phenomenon is very noticeable in Benedict's *Rule*. Matins are prayed before sunrise, and Vespers at sunset. A new day began with the evening before, just as Genesis 1:5 proclaims: "And it was evening and morning, the first day."

There are different ways of knowing, different forms of intimacy. In addition to love, suffering, sexuality, and death, prayer is a form of intimate communication and relationship with God. The night is a time for lovers, poets, and contemplatives. Our God hears our prayer since He does not sleep nor slumber (Ps 121:3-4). Therefore, we watch and pray in the watches and vigils of the night, and like sentinels waiting for daybreak, we wait for the Lord. With the dawn of sunrise, the monks recite or sing Lauds (morning praise) following the night office (Matins).

Benedict sprinkles his *Rule* and the monk's prayer life with discipline and spends a lot of time on the arrangement and ordering of the Divine Office, which begins a little past the middle of the night, one of the favorite times of a monk's prayer life. In the Middle East and Mediterranean countries of Benedict's time, the monk's Divine Office for the new day began during the wee hours of the night. Even today we monks anticipate an important feast at "First Vespers" the evening before.

What are the implications for us today? Benedict was aware of mental prayer as well as intuitive contemplative prayer, or "prayer of the heart." He suggests that we join our minds and hearts for a productive prayer life. Benedict's approach to prayer is holistic; the whole person is to participate in praising God.

When we are unable to sleep or suffer insomnia, or consciously withhold sleep, it may be a good time to practice prayer. For Benedict there is not a time of day or night, even when the monks are at work in the fields, that the psalms are absent from the monk's consciousness; this focus on the psalms translates into an awareness of God.

Praying is (or should be) as natural as breathing and as the sun's rising and setting. We breathe even when we sleep. Night time is a good time to pray. Benedict captures that virtue when he writes about the Divine Office at night.

Br. Benedict Janecko, O.S.B.

CHAPTER 9
1-11

" ... Vigils begin with the verse:
Lord, open my lips ..."

9:1

☙

AFTER THE VERY strict night silence, the words of the psalmist, "Lord, open my lips, and my mouth shall declare Your praise," seem most appropriate. It is God who should initiate our speech!

Fourteen psalms, some recited and some sung in chant, which are preceded and concluded with antiphons, constituted the Night Office in Benedict's day. Also, "responses" (answers) accompany the lessons. The monks are to "sing wisely." Only those monks who edified were chosen to sing, but as many as possible were asked to assume this duty. Pre-Gregorian chant was in vogue at the time of Benedict, but we are not sure whether he employed it. Chanting psalmody was an art which demanded training if it was to produce a "happy song" and a happy choir of monks.

The schedule of times for the Divine Office, beginning with Vigils, along with times for *lectio divina* (holy reading) and manual labor, provides a healthy, holistic rhythm of life in the monk's day. The *Rule* punctuates the monk's entire life with periods of prayer consisting mainly of the psalms from the Book of Psalms, which have been called a "school of prayer." The psalms are the "prayer book of the Bible."

As prayed by the monks along with other elements of each Hour, the psalms are called the "Work of God" (*Opus Dei*). In short, the psalms could be called the "soundtrack of our spiritual lives."

    Br. Benedict Janecko, O.S.B.

CHAPTER 10
1-3

> "But because summer nights are shorter
> the readings from the book are omitted …"
>
> 10:2

☙

When people hear a description of the monastic life, they often express surprise at the relatively early rising hour. They think that monastic life must involve a commitment to be sleep-deprived. Actually, it is the other away around. Saint Benedict used a solar calendar in which the monks went to bed with the sun, and during the long winter nights they got more than eight hours of sleep. The monks did get less sleep during the summer, but this decrease was true of everyone else in a culture where people had to "make hay while the sun shines." In the summer with its short nights, Benedict shortens Vigils by dropping the three long readings and replacing them with a short Old Testament reading recited from memory. Benedict's motivation must have been to keep the time for sleep from being excessively shortened.

Our modern, caffeinated, electricity-driven culture has trouble respecting the rhythms of our human bodies. Benedict, on the other hand, respects both the rhythms of our bodies and the yearning of our hearts to acknowledge God's presence and sing God's praises at the beginning of each day.

Fr. Nathan Munsch, O.S.B.

CHAPTER 11
1-13

"On Sunday the monks should arise earlier for Vigils."

11:1

☙

SOMETHING PRESUMED IN the *Rule* of Saint Benedict, consonant with the Christian culture at the time it was written, is that Sunday is special. In our own time, this is not as evident from either western Christian culture or secular culture. Although Sunday is part of the modern "weekend," we have lost the sense of the unique *holiness* of Sunday. We tend to treat Sunday much like any other day, except that we may also make it a day of greater self-indulgence. We give ourselves permission to sleep in, watch more sports, catch up on the week's work, or indulge in additional entertainments. This slippage of the meaning of Sunday, from holiness down into self-indulgence, can be seen in the slippage in meaning that occurred between the phrase "holy day" and the derived word "holiday." Blessed Pope John Paul II speaks beautifully about the true meaning and importance of Sunday in his apostolic letter *Dies Domini*, in which he also urges bishops and priests "to work tirelessly with the faithful to ensure that the value of this sacred day is understood and lived ever more deeply. This will bear rich fruit in Christian communities, and will not fail to have a positive influence on civil society as a whole" (#87).

From the *Rule* of Saint Benedict we can gain some insight about the meaning of Sunday and how to live it. In Chapter 11 we learn that it is a day to rise earlier for prayer, not to sleep in. Sunday is a day for more personal prayer, with a substitution of additional *lectio divina* for time that would have been spent on work (*RB* 48). Sunday is the day to begin anew: the monks begin a new cycle of prayer (*RB* 18), a new cycle of fraternal service (*RB* 35), and a new cycle of liturgical service (*RB* 38). Each Sunday is a new beginning, filled with the alleluias of Easter (*RB* 15) and marked with the qualities of the solemn festivals of the year (*RB* 14). We get up earlier on Sundays with the excitement of a child who rises early on Christmas Day, confident that God has many gifts to bestow upon us and eager to receive them as soon as possible.

Fr. Boniface Hicks, O.S.B.

CHAPTER 11
1-13

> "Let special care be taken that this [the monks' arriving late] not happen …"
>
> *11:13*

❧

Sᴜɴᴅᴀʏ, ᴛʜᴇ Lᴏʀᴅ's Day, is set apart by the Church for liturgical worship and rest in the Lord. Saint Benedict gives special attention to the celebration of the Liturgy of the Hours on Sundays; this special attention begins in Chapter 11 with the description of the Office of Vigils. Monks should arrive earlier for Vigils on Sunday than on the other days of the week. Guarding against the tendency which many follow, namely to sleep in and be less vigilant for prayer and other duties of life, this earlier rising reminds the monks of the preeminence of the Lord's Day.

While Saint Benedict speaks of moderation with respect to the quantity of the psalms and other prayers, nevertheless the requirements for Sunday Vigils are significantly more than for the Offices celebrated at other times. There is the addition of another reading after each set of six psalms; the result is that <u>eight</u>, rather than the normal six, readings will be read from the Old and New Testaments as well as from reputable orthodox Catholic Fathers. Vigils is also joyfully extended by the addition of three canticles from the prophets, of four New Testament readings, of the hymn "We Praise You, God," of the proclamation from the Gospels, and of the hymn "To You Be Praise."

At the end of the chapter, Saint Benedict warns his monks against rising too late on the Lord's Day. If such slothfulness was to occur, the readings and/or the responses would have to be shortened. He insists that special care be taken so that such behavior will not occur and specifies that monks who are responsible for such negligence must make due satisfaction in the oratory. Such attentiveness and the desire for worshiping God are at the heart of the monk's initiation into the monastic way of life. The novice, like all monks as well as all Christians, should seek God above all and, furthermore, show eagerness for the Work of God as well as for obedience and trials (*RB* 58:7). Sunday Vigils, as the weekly representation of the annual Easter Vigil, should be joyfully anticipated by all monks as the high point of their worship of God each week.

Fr. John-Mary Tompkins, O.S.B.

CHAPTER 12
1-4

> "Sunday Lauds begin with Psalm 66 [67],
> said straight through without a refrain."
>
> 12:1

☙

IF A PSALM is to be recited simply and without an antiphon, then the one praying is to listen especially closely to the text of the psalm. The antiphon, or "refrain," when used, provides a theme. The *Holy Rule* instructs us to pay attention to whatever theme emerges from Psalm 67. We recite and hear the text of this psalm and pray with it as the first word of the first day during the first Office of the first week as the sun is rising. Here is a text that helps to define the experience of morning praise. Saint Benedict seems to invite us to experience the new light of another week as a sign of the blessing of Light Divine. The gracious light of the morning sunshine is only a glimpse of the blessing we experience when the LORD lets the light of His face shine upon us.

As this Heavenly Light guides us on our way for the week ahead, truth and wisdom reveal to all the nations how we are saved. We are led out of darkness, and it becomes apparent that God is leading us on our way in life. We glow with the brightness of His Face, and it becomes hard for the people to gaze upon our face, so transformed and glorious have we become as we follow His way of salvation. This way is the way of the Cross, the way taught by the Incarnate Word, who prayed these psalms with devotion and frequency. In the promise of this first psalm of the week, we hear of the shouts of gladness of the nations as they find their way through history. As their days begin to bear the fruits of the earth, all peoples of the world are full of praise. All the ends of the earth come to hallow the Name of the LORD. The Lord Jesus, who taught us to pray "hallowed be Thy name," teaches us again in this Office to live in praise and to lead the people in boundless gladness.

Fr. Andrew Campbell, O.S.B.

CHAPTER 13
1-11

> "On other days ... a Canticle from the Prophets is said, according to the practice of the Roman Church."
>
> *13:10*

❧

IF WE READ it carefully, Chapter 13 of the *Rule* brings us a reminder of Saint Benedict's brief but formative days as a young man in Rome. He is believed to have been sent to Rome to receive a classical education, though he fled from the city after a short sojourn there since he was scandalized by the moral degradation he found. His mention of the liturgy as it was prayed in "the Roman Church"—a unique reference in the *Rule*—demonstrates that while he was in Rome, he became familiar with the liturgical practices which flourished there, even in the midst of a profane environment. Saint Benedict was thus able to take something good and edifying from a period of his life which in worldly eyes must have seemed wasted. His example should inspire us to discover and retain the goodness that is present, often in veiled ways, in events and periods of our lives which we would rather forget. In doing so, we begin to imitate Saint Benedict's humility, and we open ourselves to the grace of God, which makes goodness blossom forth even from the hardest moments of our lives.

FR. EDWARD MAZICH, O.S.B.

CHAPTER 13
12-14

> "Assuredly, the celebration of Lauds and Vespers must never pass by without the superior's reciting the entire Lord's Prayer at the end for all to hear, because thorns of contention are likely to spring up."
>
> *13:12*

☙

SAINT BENEDICT UNDERSTOOD human nature. Insisting that the Lord's Prayer be recited at the "hinge" hours of Lauds and Vespers, Benedict reminds us that we need to forgive our brothers – and seek their forgiveness – for the little slights that are part of the day.

Just as molecules cannot occupy the same space without rubbing up against each other and causing friction, neither can monks occupy the same monastery without there being some chafing of personalities throughout the day. Knowing this, Benedict legislates that we be reminded of the importance of forgiveness as we start and finish our work day. He even includes the reminder at the other hours, "but deliver us from evil" (Mt 6:13), to alert us to the temptation to be impatient with one another.

Ultimately, however, Benedict's wise reminders are only part of a greater program of ongoing conversion that gives each monk opportunities to grow. We must make the choice to respond to each opportunity by electing not to be impatient with our brothers, by forgiving quickly, and by being mindful of the needs of others so as not to be a deliberate source of irritation to them. As always, Benedict guides, but we must choose to accept his guidance.

Fr. Philip Kanfush, O.S.B.

CHAPTER 14
1-2

"On the feasts of saints ... the Sunday order of celebration is followed ..."

14:1

☙

SAINT BENEDICT SHOWS us in this passage that he wants us to celebrate the saints, our brothers and sisters in heaven, in the same way we celebrate Christ, the one who sanctifies us. The feasts of saints are celebrated as true Sundays – *dies domini*" (the Lord's Day) – because those feasts are usually celebrated on the day of their deaths, or "passover" (passage) into heaven, the day when they were born to true life in heaven.

Sanctity is nothing more than developing a more intense and deeper likeness to Christ Himself. We are saintly to the extent that we become united with Him through returning His love, obeying His words, and imitating His works.

The saints of our tradition are those who lived their lives according to these precepts and, for this reason, reached the glory of heaven. Therefore, we celebrate their "passover" in the same manner in which we celebrate Sunday each week – the weekly Passover – and thus make it clear that Christ's life, Passion, Death, Resurrection, and Ascension are renewed in the members of his Body. This is the case for the saints, and this is the case for each one of us who seeks to imitate, follow, and love the Lord Jesus Christ.

FR. PAULO PANZA, O.S.B.

CHAPTER 15
1-4

> " 'Alleluia' is never said with responsories except from Easter to Pentecost."
>
> *15:4*

❦

IN THIS SHORT chapter, Saint Benedict regulates the times for saying *Alleluia,* which means "Praise the Lord!", during community prayer. Why is Benedict so concerned about limiting the use of such a magnificent word? It is because he knew the tremendous meaning *Alleluia* signifies when it is voiced at the proper time and in the proper place. He was probably very aware that the only occurrence of *Alleluia* in the New Testament is in Chapter 19 of the Book of Revelation (19:1, 3, 4, 6), which describes the wedding feast of the Lamb. This feast is the triumphal banquet at which all the souls redeemed by Christ unceasingly praise God for His salvation. For Benedict, life at the monastery was supposed to be a foretaste of this life in heaven, symbolized by the wedding feast of the Lamb. Therefore, in anticipation of heavenly life, Benedict might have thought, "If we will be unceasingly acclaiming *Alleluia* when we are in heaven, how could we not also acclaim it, in proper measure, while we are still exiles here on earth?" Clearly Benedict knew and loved the beauty of this word. However, he also recognized that, as lowly and sinful exiles, we have yet to attain the blessed life of full communion with God. Therefore, the most appropriate times for saying *Alleluia* are related to the times when we most vividly remember the Resurrection: the entire season of Easter; the hour of Vigils, that is, early in the morning and the time of day in which Christ rose from the dead; and Sunday, the day of the Resurrection.

Br. Canice McMullen, O.S.B.

CHAPTER 16
1-5

> "Therefore, we should *praise* our Creator
> *for his just judgments* at these times ..."
>
> 16:5

☙

Monks of Saint Benedict's day were to pray in community eight times a day (if Vigils is counted); yes, not *seven* but *eight*! This would be a daunting regime of prayer for nearly anyone, but there must be a reason for turning to God so frequently. Aside from a historical reason, we could also posit a more intimate reason. With some help from Benedict, the same psalm with which the practice of eight offices is justified provides this reason. According to Benedict's use of Psalm 119, we are to turn to God so that we might praise Him for His "*just judgments*" (Psalm 119:164). This psalm is an exceptionally long meditation on God's Law. Drawing from this psalm, I take God's just judgments to mean the "rules" He has set down according to which life might be lived happily. Having knowledge of such judgments naturally gives rise to joy, a joy that would ideally lead to a desire to praise the One from Whom they have come. Aside from the joy of knowing God's ways, these judgments also give rise to the desire for assistance in carrying them out. For both of these reasons we in the present age ought to turn to God as often as we are able, even if we are unable to pray eight times a day.

Br. Matthew Lambert, O.S.B.

CHAPTER 17
1-10

> "If the community is rather large, refrains are used with the psalms; if it is smaller, the psalms are said without refrain."
>
> *17:6*

☙☛

IN READING CHAPTERS 8 to 18 of the *Rule*, one might be overwhelmed by Saint Benedict's attention to detail in specifying how each of the Hours of community prayer was to be carried out. We should understand that Saint Benedict <u>was</u> attentive to details, but not in a fanatic way nor with the intention of imposing his arrangement on future generations. He obviously loved the Divine Office as a major vehicle of praising God and of being in contact with God; and when one loves, one is careful about details that will express one's love and please the beloved, especially when the Beloved is God Himself.

Furthermore, it is important to realize that Saint Benedict was following a tradition of praying that was inherited through generations of monastic tradition. Although that tradition was reliable and time-tested, he also allowed for modifications and adaptations (see *RB* 18:22). In this chapter he says that smaller communities need not use refrains (usually called "antiphons" today) at Terce, Sext, and None (and presumably at Prime, too). Perhaps the reason was that a small group would find it difficult to chant antiphons.

Here at St. Vincent our Divine Office is significantly different from that specified in the *Rule*. We officially gather as a community for the Liturgy of the Hours three times a day.

We use no antiphons at Vigils (except on solemnities and feasts) or at Midday Prayer. Also, the arrangement of our Office is considerably different than it was when I entered the monastery in 1977. I think it is a big improvement, partly because recent changes have tried to recapture some of the authentic tradition that was too hastily cast away after Vatican Council II.

We can all learn something from Saint Benedict's adherence to tradition and his adaptation of tradition. All Christians are committed to embrace a sacred tradition based on God's revelation in the Bible and most especially in the Passion, Death, and Resurrection of Christ. Certain elements of this tradition are based on absolute truths that come from God and cannot be changed, despite our culture's tendency to question everything and to render nothing absolute. The Eucharist in the Catholic Church, for example, would not be valid without certain essential elements that form part of our Sacred Tradition.

On the other hand, some practices of Christian tradition, based on human decisions, are open to adaptation. Neither God nor the Church has specified how the psalms must be recited (although the "Roman Office" and monastic documents from Rome provide very significant norms). Besides, every tradition, no matter how valid, can become empty unless we make it a part of our personal journey of faith. A slavish, impersonal following of a tradition, sometimes called "traditionalism," can make one self-righteous in clinging to the details of ritual. In contrast, authentic tradition is the Spirit-filled embracing of what has been passed on by our ancestors in the faith. The point of all religious tradition is to bring us closer to God. Let us all learn to pray the Divine Office in a way that respects the tradition of the Church and yet allows us to encounter Christ personally and to welcome Him to touch our hearts.

Fr. Donald Raila, O.S.B.

CHAPTER 18
1-6

"… Sunday Vigils [should] always begin with Psalm 20 [21]."

18:6

☙

ONE OF THE treasures of following a liturgical cycle of readings and psalms is that God's Word is prepared for us ahead of time and awaits our encounter with Him at the "favorable time," on the "day of salvation." Adhering to such a fixed cycle that has been passed down to us, we surrender to God, in a very practical way, our control over how He will present Himself to us. If we have ears to hear what the Spirit is speaking to the Churches when we regularly recite the psalms while praying the Liturgy of the Hours and when we reflect upon the readings of the Office and Mass, we shall discover that His Word shapes and changes us in His time, in His way, and according to His will, not ours. We shall also begin to realize that He not only prepares His Word to meet us in the official liturgy of the Church, but that His Word has also been sent ahead of us to be encountered and received during the "liturgy" of our daily lives. The events of everyday life thus become opportunities for us to surrender our will and be transformed by the power of the living Word of God.

FR. SHAWN MATTHEW ANDERSON, O.S.B.

CHAPTER 18
7-11

"On Monday at Terce, Sext and None, the nine remaining sections of Psalm 118 [119] are said …"

18:7

☙

Psalm 119 is taken up as a kind of refrain for praying the rest of the Psalms. It celebrates the glory of God and of His law. It repeats such words as "blessed are those who do not forget Your law, who keep Your precepts." The psalmist prays to be faithful and steadfast and promises to keep God's statutes. He meditates in his heart; he seeks with all his heart; he praises God with his lips; and he fixes his eyes on Him. The psalmist delights, is consumed with longing, melts away with sorrow, and clings to God. He knows the Lord's faithfulness and is confirmed in His mercy. He rediscovers His righteousness and delights in the Lord time and again, with the gift of knowing that the Lord's love is forever!

Perhaps we can say that this psalm summarizes all the other psalms and leads us through all the moments of our search for God. It does not allow us to forget, refuels us when we are empty, and helps us remember. It is like a much-repeated refrain (using various words) in the Opus Dei because it brings us again and again to the surprises of God and to our capacity to delight in the Lord. These dispositions allow us to meet Him over and over again in our daily lives, to find Him when we have strayed from Him, and to remember Him when we have forgotten Him.

Fr. Thomas Acklin, O.S.B.

CHAPTER 18
12-19

"This is the order of psalms for Vespers ..."

18:18

☙

IN THIS SECTION of the *Rule* we are given yet additional proof of Saint Benedict's practicality, prudence, and thoughtful structuring in what he gives to those desiring to follow Christ. Here, in writing about the structure of Vespers (Evening Prayer), he gives an order to the Psalms prayed: *Digesto ergo ordine psalmorum vespertinorum* (cf. *RB* 18:18).

Pope Emeritus Benedict XVI wrote that the Liturgy of the Hours sanctifies the entirety of the day and gives it "rhythm" through the hearing of the word of God and the recitation of the Psalms and thus imbues everything with "praise offered to God" (cf. *Verbum Domini*, 62).

Regardless of one's state in life or situation, the Liturgy of the Hours helps one grow in one's capacity to walk with God. This "service" to God, as experienced in praying the Office, is both ecclesial and individual; it enables one to serve others and "become part of the Church's great pilgrimage through history until the end of the world" (cf. Pope Francis, *Lumen Fidei*, 22).

Thus, in structuring Evening Prayer, Saint Benedict helps us fall into a healthful rhythm and frees us to listen to God as He speaks to us, with the result that we have the strength to serve those whom God has placed in our lives.

FREDERICK A. LAUX

CHAPTER 18
20-25

"... if anyone finds this distribution of the psalms unsatisfactory, he should arrange whatever he judges better, provided that the full complement of one hundred and fifty psalms is by all means carefully maintained every week ..."

18:22-23

☙

As TWENTY-FIRST CENTURY Christians, we may find it hard to believe that the church of Jesus Christ existed without having rich hymnody to sing. How, we imagine, did these believers get by without ever singing "Amazing Grace"? Yet for centuries – yes, centuries! – the Church's song was composed exclusively of psalms, chanted and or paraphrased. It was, after all, the song book of the Hebrews, chronicling many of the political and religious experiences of God's people; it remains so for the Jews today.

Benedict was quite particular that the entire Psalter be sung or recited over the course of a week. Onerous as this regimen may have seemed to some, his insistence really was a gift to all who follow the *Rule*, since it would otherwise be easy to say or sing only those psalms which suit us or make us comfortable. Who, after all, is thrilled about adding dulcet tones to Psalm 137, for example? We don't like to talk (or sing) about assaulting children, but it is good that we keep such psalms in our repertoire, if for no other reason than to remind us of how healthy it is to express visceral feelings about our own story.

We who are Oblates may find it challenging to take on even a monthly recitation of the complete Psalter, "in so far as our state in life permits," but we can marvel at, and give thanks for, the discipline of those who praise God with His own Word so fully.

The Rev. Dr. Jeff Loach

CHAPTER 19
1-7

> "But beyond the least doubt we should believe this [that the divine presence is everywhere] to be especially true when we celebrate the divine office."
>
> 19:2

☙

THE MONK PUNCTUATES each day with periods of prayer, composed mainly of psalmody, and like so many aspects of monastic life, this has to be learned. It is truly a discipline, similar to that of an athlete who is in training and is striving for perfection.

The "Discipline of Psalmody," treated particularly in this chapter, really pertains to all of Chapters 8 through 20, since the arrangement, selection, number, and singing of the psalms, as well as reverence for the psalms, whether on a festive day or an ordinary day, all demand discipline. Benedict is very meticulous when it comes to his discussion of psalmody, which we could call "150 steps between life and death." For the monk, then and now, psalmody is the soundtrack and lifeline of his journey with God and with his confreres.

The monk's day is sprinkled with psalms of lament and of praise, which echo the Death and Resurrection of Jesus, whom we might call the "monk par excellence." There is not a time at day or night or a time while one is at work in the fields that the psalms are absent from the monk's consciousness.

By way of analogy, in his book *Fear No Evil*, Natan (Anatoly) Sharansky, a Russian dissident, relates how the Book of Psalms, a wedding gift from his wife, became his lifeline during his nine years of incarceration. His discipline in studying and praying the psalms during this ordeal kept him sane and also maintained his contact with his wife and with God. This story shows how the psalms can benefit the monk and Oblate alike.

In Chapter 49 Benedict speaks of a monk's life as a continual Lent; that means that a monk requires ongoing discipline. Praying and working are disciplines, just as Lent and life itself are disciplines, that is, learning processes involved with discipleship. This discipline overflows into the praying of psalmody: arriving on time, and praying with humility and with devotion, since we are in the presence of God and His angels. (Thus Chapter 19 seems to continue the degrees of humility in Chapter 7.) Indeed, humility is the pillar upon which Benedict builds his *Rule* and his recommendations for a prayer life.

Br. Benedict Janecko, O.S.B.

CHAPTER 19
1-7

"... and let us stand to sing the psalms in such a way that our minds are in harmony with our voices."

19:7

☙

THE ANCIENT HEBREW psalms of David express the heart of man, the heart of the Church, and the heart of prayer. The psalms provide access to God, the Creator of all. They are an expression of a praying Church. Also, they share life-experiences. Sometimes they reach into the abyss; at other times they display ecstasy. They voice praise, intercession, adoration, thanksgiving, petition, and reflection, as well as so much more. When we pray the psalms, we unite ourselves universally to the rest of God's people. The Divine Office is prayed at all times of the day throughout the world.

When we pray the psalms, we draw ever closer to God and come to know what He is trying to teach us and provide for us. He encourages, teaches, leads, consoles, and warns. Regular and timely recitation of the psalms provides a holy path of life for us pilgrims as it did for the Israelites in David's time. It is with humility that we approach these ancient prayers. It is with reverence and holy fear that we pray as we ought; Saint Paul tells us, "In the same way, the Spirit too comes to the aid of our weakness; for we do not know how to pray as we ought, but the Spirit itself intercedes with inexpressible groanings. And the one who searches hearts knows what is the intention of the Spirit" (Rom 8: 26-27). We approach the Divine as creature to Creator. We wait on Him. We seek to be given the grace needed to lift our hearts and voices in faith. We trust that He is always present. In response to Him, we try to be fully present in mind, body, and spirit and thus show our love for God, who has loved us first. (cf. Ps 135:3: "Sing a psalm to His name for He is loving.")

Sr. Marie Teresa Tellier, C.H.

CHAPTER 20
1-5

"[We are to] lay our petitions before the Lord God of all things with the utmost humility and sincere devotion."

20:2

☙

THIS INSTRUCTION ON "reverence in prayer" requires us, first of all, to have certain dispositions: humility, devotion, purity of heart, and tears of compunction. First, when we pray, we must approach Him with humility and devotion because these are the dispositions with which God approached us; in humility God took on human flesh and became man, and in devotion to us He poured out His life for the sake of our salvation. Therefore, it is in humility that we come to God as people who have been redeemed at the cost of His life, and it is in devotion that we offer ourselves wholly to Him as people who seek to do His will in response to His love.

Secondly, Saint Benedict tells us that God does not judge our prayers by their length but by our "purity of heart and tears of compunction" (20:3). Jesus said, "Blessed are the pure of heart, for they shall see God" (Mt 5:8). When man is blinded by worldly desire, he cannot "see God," but when his heart solely desires God, he approaches Him with the reverence due to Him alone.

Finally, reverence in prayer is helped by tears of compunction. Tears indicate that we have been touched by grace. They are both tears of sorrow for our sins and tears of joy for the salvation that has been won for us, unworthy though we are.

BR. CANICE MCMULLEN, O.S.B.

CHAPTER 21
1-7

"[The deans] are to be chosen for virtuous living and wise teaching, not for their rank."

21:4

☙

OBEDIENCE AND HUMILITY are at the center of the *Rule*, and Chapter 21 is one of several chapters where Saint Benedict applies these principles to leadership. A hallmark of Christian life (and of monastic life in particular) is that divine authority is mediated through visible structures. Through God's providence imperfect human beings are entrusted with God's own authority so that they become, in a sense, a sacrament of His presence. This is the honor but also the burden which the abbot shares with his officials called "deans." This authority may be shared only with those of "good repute and holy life" (21:1), without respect to rank alone. No one is *owed* the honor of leadership, including those who hold the office. A good leader must ever recall verse 29 of the Prologue: "these people fear the Lord, and do not become elated over their good deeds; they judge it is the Lord's power, not their own, that brings about the good in them."

The humble realize that God is the source of all their good; if they are called to leadership, it is so that these gifts may be spent in the service of others. Proud leaders mistakenly believe that their power exists for their own sake. Though here Saint Benedict does not quote Christ's words that "the greatest among you must be your servant," they certainly apply. In Christian leadership one's position should not "go to one's head"; rather it should inspire a more fervent prayer life and a more generous living of the Gospel. The one called to service, ever aware of his own weakness, must recognize that he is no longer responsible for himself only, but also for those placed in his care. Whether our role in life is to lead or to follow, we always need humility in order to place God's agenda first, and we need a willing obedience to our superiors since it is through them that His will is expressed.

Br. Lawrence Machia, O.S.B.

CHAPTER 22
1-8

"A lamp must be kept burning in the room until morning."

22:4

☙

SOME DETAILS OF this chapter are no longer practiced in most contemporary monasteries, but we can still derive insight from the attitudes prescribed by Saint Benedict in this section of the *Rule*. According to Blessed Columba Marmion, the key note for the whole *Rule* of Saint Benedict is that "the divine presence is everywhere" (*RB* 19:1). Night time stirs up a special temptation against this truth. At night we tend to be alone and undisturbed, even hidden from sight by the darkness. We can distort this tendency into a sense that even God cannot see what we are doing, and this illusion can give rise to sins of self-absorption or self-indulgence.

To the contrary, Saint Benedict cultivates a different attitude in the hearts of his monks. He cultivates an attitude of watchfulness. Night time, for Saint Benedict, is not a time to collapse into self-indulgence or merely to decompress from the day's activities. Night time is, rather, a time to look forward to the beginning of a new day with a lamp kept burning, with a readiness to engage that new day. Because the unconsciousness of sleep is the closest we come each day to death, when we lay down our bodies at the end of the day, Saint Benedict teaches us to make an act of hope as we look forward to the opportunity to rise again for prayer. In this way our falling asleep, our sleeping, and our remaining in "readiness to arise without delay" all become acts of prayer and faith-filled affirmations that the "divine presence is everywhere." These dimensions of sleep express our willingness to entrust our lives entirely to God.

Fr. Boniface Hicks, O.S.B.

CHAPTER 23
1-5

"If a brother is found to be stubborn or disobedient or proud ..."

23:1

☙

My first encounter with Chapter 23 led me to focus not so much on a literal interpretation of the punitive measures for those who have committed faults but rather on the ways we sometimes *unjustly* excommunicate others through our thoughts, words, or deeds. At times our response to others' faults is to bypass the first steps of private admonition mandated by Benedict, and instead to gossip about them, give them the "cold shoulder," or harbor uncharitable thoughts about them. In these ways, we sow discord in the community (workplace, family, parish, etc.) and may even cause irreparable damage to the spirit of fraternity.

I appreciate Benedict's insistence that we examine our motives and keep our unhealthy ones in check: are my choices helping to build up or tear down the Kingdom? If I am tempted to gossip or keep people in their sins or harbor negative thoughts about them, I should ask myself if I should not rather be helping them in their time of weakness. Or am I more concerned with making myself look better? What is really going on inside of myself? Our concern should be always to build a climate of merciful love!

Pauline Lanciotti

CHAPTER 24
1-7

"The measure of excommunication or of chastisement should correspond to the degree of fault …"

24:1; Leonard J. Doyle trans.

☙

MANY SCHOLARS OF the *Holy Rule* assert that Saint Benedict seems to have been maturing as an abbot throughout his writing of the document. In Chapter 24 we can read a certain level of kindness and mercy in the "manner of excommunication." First of all, we should note that excommunication is not the only punishment. The text reads, "excommunication or punishment." Some failures demand excommunication, and others incur only a lesser kind of punishment.

Sometimes a monk has already separated himself from the community by consistent and malicious behavior. The very presence of such a monk is poisonous to the other monks, and such a monk must be removed before he damages others with his bad example. If, however, a monk is unfaithful to his vow of *conversatio morum* on just one occasion and learns from that experience of failure and forgiveness, his humble and penitential life will be a shining example, and he should not be excommunicated. Only the abbot determines the degree of harshness of any necessary corrective measures. This provision, too, is a sign of mercy and kindness because it is the abbot who knows most about the interior life of the monk and can put things into proper perspective. The abbot also has a vested interest in how the monk appropriates his correction and penance. Indeed, the

115

abbot is warned to scrape the rust off the vessel <u>gently</u> so as not to make a hole (cf. *RB* 64:12).

Saint Benedict is careful to keep the offending monk away from public function until he has made the necessary satisfaction. This isolation will prevent any resentment from arising during any oral interpretation that could be heard in a monk's intoning a psalm or antiphon or in his reading in the oratory. The offending monk is also kept from taking his meals with the rest of the community so that he does not distract the brothers from prayer during the silence of their common meals. Just his sitting at table with a smiling or somber face could draw attention to his punishment. Saint Benedict, in his wisdom, gives the offending monk the kind of solitude necessary to enter fully into a conversion through repentance—at a deep heart level. Indeed, it is not enough to say, "I'm sorry." Each repentant monk needs to *feel* regret and to desire to acquire a change of heart and behavior. Again it is mercy and kindness that the *Holy Rule* demands of the abbot when he is dealing with the weaknesses or failures of his monks—the very same mercy and kindness that the abbot has first received from the Lord God.

Fr. Andrew Campbell, O.S.B.

CHAPTER 25
1-6

"He will work alone at the tasks assigned to him, living continually in sorrow and penance ..."

25:3

☙

SAINT BENEDICT WRITES at length about different kinds of faults and the redress that should accompany them. In Chapter 25 he turns to the most serious faults, those which risk fracturing the very order on which the life of the monastic community rests and thus jeopardize the possibility that monks will be able to live meaningful and productive lives in search of God. Saint Benedict instructs that these offenders be isolated from the rest of the community, much in the same way that Saint Paul ordered his flock in Corinth to isolate their wayward brethren (see 1 Cor 5). Ultimately these measures are not intended to be punitive, but rather to provide the time and space needed for true reconciliation and healing to take place. As can be seen in the following chapters in the *Rule*, Benedict exemplifies the spirit of Christ, the divine physician of souls, who came to save not the righteous but sinners. May we do likewise in dealing with our own loved ones and fellow Christians who have wronged us, so that they too "may be saved on the day of the Lord" (*RB* 25:4, 1 Cor 5:5).

FR. EDWARD MAZICH, O.S.B.

CHAPTER 26
1-2

> "If a brother ... presumes to associate ... with an excommunicated brother..., he should receive a like punishment ..."
>
> *26:1-2*

☙

AT FIRST GLANCE this provision, like some others in the *Rule*, sounds harsh and unjust. Why should a monk be punished for associating, presumably out of compassion, with another monk who has been "excommunicated" (that is, excluded from the common table or also from service in the oratory as described in 13:23-25)? Should not a fellow Christian show kind solicitude toward offenders?

Chapter 27 indicates that the abbot and community ought indeed to exhibit compassion toward offenders. However, the display of compassion must be done at the right time and in the right way. One who "presumes to associate" without permission from the abbot might very well be interfering with the established healing process, which takes time. The excommunicated monk needs to have the seriousness of his fault sink into his conscience. It is not genuinely helpful to forestall the process by conversing with him or sending him a message when he really needs some isolation to help him to repent on a deep level.

What lesson can we in this present age learn from this stipulation in our present age? Although monasteries today do not practice this form of excommunication, we can all grow in discernment of how and when to approach people who are hurting or who have seriously hurt others. Sometimes we can deceive ourselves into thinking that we are helping. We may think that we are showing compassion, but we may really be indulging in our "need to be needed." While we may exert effort to make an offender "feel good," he may benefit most from some therapeutic isolation. In order to show authentic compassion that will really help another on his or her spiritual journey, we must listen to the voice of God, examine our consciences, and heed the time-tried norms of our families or communities and *then* approach the offender, not according to our impulses but according to God's all-wise timing for helping the person to experience heartfelt conversion. Such self-restraint is also a matter of humility. What I think is right for another person may not be what is actually best. I must deal with others not according to my whims but according to time-tested norms that are ultimately given by God.

Fr. Donald Raila, O.S.B.

CHAPTER 27
1-9

"The abbot must exercise the utmost care
and concern for wayward brothers ..."

27:1

༄

THIS CHAPTER LAYS out a thoughtful, effective process for dealing with wayward monks who have been excommunicated (in a way defined by the *Rule*). The abbot, the spiritual father of the monastery, is called to be like a "wise physician" in healing spiritual wounds. He knows that those who misbehave may need a healthy dose of discipline but that, even more, they ultimately must receive consolation and compassion. The aim is not so much to punish the monk but to help him repent. The goal must be to restore the wavering monk to spiritual health, to reintegration with the community, and to a renewed relationship with Christ. Therefore, the abbot is called to imitate Christ the Good Shepherd in administering discipline; he is not to seek to bolster his own authority or to gratify himself in any way.

What can these principles mean for us today? Parents, teachers, spiritual guides, and other people with authority usually have to deal with one or more problematic people. The one with authority may be tempted to ignore the miscreants completely or to show them disdain for their lack of cooperation. Saint Benedict says, "No! Do not give in to your natural impulses. Do whatever you can to bring them back to Christ, to the Church, and to the local community or family. You must be like Christ in order to draw them back to Christ and Christ-centered behavior." Any authority must humbly be aware of his own frailty so that he may resist the tendency to put others down in order to display power. Serving the wayward is a sacred ministry. One must deal with them as God Himself deals with us.

Fr. Donald Raila, O.S.B.

CHAPTER 28
1-8

"... let him receive a sharper punishment ... so that the Lord, who can do all things, may bring about the health of the sick brother."

28:1, 5

☙

I HAVE HEARD it said that a monastery is like a hospital for spiritually sick people who want to get well. Of course, we are <u>all</u> spiritually ill and in need of redemption, but monks make it a very intentional goal to be purified of sinful tendencies and so prepare to encounter God ever more fully, both on this earth and ultimately in heaven. Through the vow of *conversatio morum*, we monks ideally welcome whatever enables us to grow closer to the Lord, however painful. Therefore, Saint Benedict specifies therapy for his "patients"; that is, he offers various therapeutic penalties that are best suited to a given offender.

The penalties mentioned in the *Rule* sound harsh to us today, but they were moderate for Saint Benedict's day. Besides, they were meant to be <u>therapeutic</u>. Note how in *RB* 28:2-3 Saint Benedict uses medical terms: "wise physician," "compresses," "ointment," "medicine," and "cauterizing iron," "health," and "amputation." All these remedies are intended to bring the wavering brother back to wholeness and, if at all possible, to preserve his monastic vocation without harming the vocation of others. Only after a succession of well-ministered remedies have failed, the last of which is an especially intense form of public prayer, is a monk to be expelled from the monastery.

Christ tells us that progress in life advancing toward the Kingdom of God is like entering a "narrow gate." All of us have sinful tendencies that need to be overcome before we meet God in His fullness; all of us need graces flowing from the sacraments and from other people's concern and prayers to assist us in spiritual growth. Likewise, we are all called in various ways to come to the aid of wavering sisters and brothers and so to enable them to move toward spiritual wholeness. Let us, with the help of Saint Benedict and the *Rule*, discern carefully the means we use to shepherd back to a living faith those who have strayed.

Fr. Donald Raila, O.S.B.

CHAPTER 29
1-3

"Let him be received back, but as a test of his humility he should be given the last place."

29:2

☙

SAINT BENEDICT INTENDS his monks to live a life centered on Christ and His Gospel. Christ Himself brought mercy and forgiveness to everyone He met who repented of wrongdoing, no matter how great the sins seemed to others. Sometimes even the apostles were harsh in judging, and Christ had to reprove them. This short chapter gives a concrete example of mercy: the one who leaves is to be received back, no matter how bad the circumstances or dramatic the departure, provided only that he repent of his action and make amends. Wouldn't that brother, we might think, be a huge liability for the community? What if he leaves again? Is he really going to be a reliable brother? Saint Benedict does not even consider any of these possibilities, but only the need to forgive and receive the brother back, even up to a third time.

Such magnanimity begs the question from us: do *we* forgive those who do us wrong? Are we able to find it in our hearts to give them another chance, or do we cut others off at the slightest offense? Without mutual forgiveness, it is impossible for us to grow as a Christian community of faith and charity.

BR. MICHAEL ANTONACCI, O.S.B.

CHAPTER 30
1-3

"... they should be subjected to severe fasts or checked with sharp strokes so that they may be healed."

30:3

❧

THIS CHAPTER OF the *Rule* seems to supplement other chapters that stress the importance of ready and quick obedience to God and to one's superiors in order to nurture steady, consistent spiritual growth and maturity in one's love for God and for others. Saint Benedict recognizes, however, that some individuals, especially "boys and the young," may not fully understand the serious consequences of disobedience, which can lead to being "excommunicated" (i.e., deprived of full participation in meals and/or communal prayer) from the school of the Lord's service. Such people, by their clinging to self-will, may incur delays and impediments on the journey to eternal salvation. Therefore, Saint Benedict aptly points out the need for increased discipline for repeated infractions.

Although these measures may sound severe to our modern mentality, they represent Saint Benedict's awareness of the urgent need for monks' continual conversion in order for them to advance on the way of eternal salvation (cf. Prol: 48-49). Saint Benedict's keen insight about the shortness of time we have in life to please God and to prepare ourselves to live with Him forever is apparent in the disciplinary measures that he specifies, even for those who are young. He is eager to help his monks to grow continually in self-awareness, obedience, and the love of God and of others. Thus the monk – and the lay person who undertakes the appropriate disciplines for himself or herself – progresses toward experiencing the eternal beatitude that awaits those who persevere in faith. God Himself, who is total love, wants no less for us than to know His love completely, as much as possible on this earth and certainly in fullness hereafter.

LINDA ROCKEY

CHAPTER 31
1-12

"He will regard all utensils and goods of the monastery as sacred vessels of the altar ..."

31:10

ଧ

THE *RULE* OF Saint Benedict is relentlessly practical and is filled with mundane details of how a monastic community is to be organized. One such seemingly routine administrative detail is addressed in these verses, which describe the qualifications of the community's business manager (the "cellarer") and specify how he is to care for and deploy the monastery's property.

However, in the midst of this administrative "fine print" Saint Benedict radically reframes the cellarer's responsibilities by requiring that he "regard all utensils and goods of the monastery as sacred vessels of the altar" (31:10). Thus the tools of the cellarer's trade are not mere means for feeding and sheltering the community; they are *instruments of blessing*.

We live in a material world and are stewards of countless items that assist us in carrying out our responsibilities and stewardships. By approaching these items as "sacred vessels of the altar," we not only affirm the goodness of God's creation but also acknowledge the holiness inherent in all of our work. This perspective enables us to work as diligently as Martha while we maintain a heart like Mary's (cf. Lk 10:38-42) – a heart that in the midst of life's busyness can nevertheless remain undivided in its loving attentiveness to Christ.

REV. SCOTT E. SCHUL

CHAPTER 31
1-12

> "As cellarer of the monastery, there should be chosen from the community someone who is wise, mature in conduct, ... God-fearing, and like a father to the whole community."
>
> *31:1-2*

☙

Reflecting on these verses, I had a strong impression that the described qualifications could also be attributed to the personal qualities of Saint Joseph. God would require the highest character and abilities for the protector of the Holy Family; therefore, the virtues of the cellarer would necessarily have been part of Saint Joseph's character.

Saint Joseph was obedient to God in fulfilling his earthly mission just as the cellarer is obedient to the abbot. Saint Joseph would have been responsible for the practical operation of the Holy Family's home and for the well-being of others in the community at Nazareth, just as the cellarer ought to be concerned about the monks of the monastery as well as guests and the poor who come to the door. On a daily basis Saint Joseph would have demonstrated wisdom in quietly fulfilling his work and his divine mission. This quiet and faithful service manifests true strength. The cellarer is called to fulfill his duties in the same manner. It is a tall order for any person, but with the grace of God it is possible to incorporate these virtues, whether one lives in a monastery or outside. The qualifications of the cellarer are a good place for all of us to look for virtues to imitate and in which to grow over the course of a lifetime.

James "Jay" Wells

CHAPTER 31
13-19

"Above all, let him be humble."

31:13

☙

IN HIS CHAPTER on the cellarer of the monastery, Saint Benedict again demonstrates his knowledge of the human condition. The cellarer is the monk to whom is entrusted the care of, and responsibility for, all of the temporalities of the monastery. In comparison with other jobs in the monastery, this role gives the incumbent monk access to considerable resources, and so it is important that he be one who understands who he is before God. Others may envy his position, or even attempt to exploit it; but lest he cause others any discomfort, the cellarer must be humble and patient in the face of all situations.

Saint Benedict admonishes the cellarer to have a kind word for those whose requests he cannot accommodate. Such a response is particularly important because very often such requests come at inopportune times, when he might be tired or inclined toward impatience. If the cellarer has to make an error in his dealings with the brothers, let that error be on the side of generosity.

What is true of the cellarer is true for any of us. We all are called upon to respond to others' demands. Gentleness, patience and humility are always appropriate responses.

FR. PHILIP KANFUSH, O.S.B.

CHAPTER 31
13-19

> "He should take care of all that the abbot entrusts to him ..."
>
> *31:15*

☙

OUR EYES PAN over material possessions from a lifetime together, from a home and family now scattered around the country. My husband and I wonder together, "What shall we do with all these things? Who, in this large family, should be given which items, and where should the remainder be donated?" In pondering these things, I am reminded of the *Rule* and how our father Benedict tells us to be humble as we distribute items.

How many times have you looked at items to be donated and simply wanted to get them out the way? Careful consideration of the needs of others will lead to respectful distribution of gently used items. Recycling centers will take electronics, chemicals, and many other household goods. Charities that collect for those caught in abject poverty will accept clothes, furniture, and working appliances. Most of all, we must honor the wishes of the ones to whom all these things once belonged. We are simply their hands as we pack for future generations sentimental treasures, needed household items, and clothes and as we work to preserve our environment by properly recycling unwanted materials. Ultimately, all these things belong to God, and it is to Him that we are responsible as we dispose of them.

Working together, detaching ourselves from things, and attaching ourselves to God alone, we can accomplish our earthly goals in a timely fashion and avoid aggravations along the way. We can thus also cooperate in God's own plan for the careful disposition of material things.

Sandra L. Monier

CHAPTER 32
1-5

"Whoever fails to keep the things belonging to the monastery clean or treats them carelessly should be reproved."

32:4

☙

We have been truly blessed by the wonders of this world, which are gifts from God. Walk down the street, and there is an abundance of food surrounding us: from stuffed grocery stores to overflowing, fruit-filled trees; from crunchy garden harvests to fresh juice-dripping berries on wild berry bushes. All of these are resources for our bodies provided by God. We see the iron ore turned into steel cars puttering down the street; we see heavier-than-bird, new-age fibrous planes miraculously ascending into the sky as if lighter than a bird; we see tree-felled lumber turned into boats floating across the lake with the fish. All of these are tools for living provided by God.

We are stewards of these wonders, these tools, with which the Lord has blessed us. We must use them wisely and for the benefit of all. Since these are God's gifts and proofs of His love for all of us, careless use of these is a rejection of His love.

Lora Anne Jacob

CHAPTER 33
1-8

"Above all, this evil practice [private ownership] must be uprooted and removed from the monastery."

33:1

☙

ONE OF SAINT Benedict's strongest admonitions in the *Rule* is aimed at personal possessions. An immediate reaction to the ban on this might be the sense that a large part of one's freedom is being taken away. In reality, however, the lack of private ownership grants the monastic greater freedom by removing the need for procuring, maintaining, and protecting material items. As stated in the book *Lessons from St. Benedict*, "In the paradox of the cross, earthy loss becomes a joyful gain of heavenly pleasure!" The giving up of earthly possessions grants the monastic the freedom to pursue Christ with one's whole heart.

We Oblates, on the other hand, do not have the option of possessing nothing. We must find a way of providing ourselves with the necessities of shelter, food, and clothing. Once these things are secured, we are obligated to maintain and protect them; sometimes in this process we may wonder whether we actually possess the material goods or *are possessed* by them. When we choose to increase our holdings, we also choose to increase the time we must allot for their care. With a larger house, for example, comes the burden not only of additional cost and increased time and expense of maintenance, but also greater need for protection commensurate with the higher monetary value. These demands decrease our freedom in the use of time and money. The time and treasure that are expended on material goods might be better spent in the pursuit of a deepening relationship with Christ.

How, then, can we apply Chapter 33 to our lives as Oblates? First of all, we can accept that, in reality, we own <u>nothing</u>. The home to which we hold a deed will ultimately pass over to someone else; the "dream car" that we are driving will finally wear out and have to be replaced; and one can be sure that our newest electronic device will quickly become outdated and then simply must be relegated to the junk drawer when a newer version is acquired.

Only when we become truly aware that we are just caretakers of material goods can we view them as items meant to fulfill our real needs as opposed to our wants. When we begin to question whether we actually need a planned purchase, whether we can simplify our lives, and whether our sense of value is appropriate concerning worldly goods, then we are starting to apply this wisdom from the *Rule* to our lives. Furthermore, the freedom to offer our time and treasure to the Lord will increase proportionately to the degree that we are able to surrender our sense of ownership in the spirit of these precepts from Saint Benedict.

Paul Fling

CHAPTER 34
1-7

> "Whoever needs less should thank God and not be distressed, but whoever needs more should feel humble because of his weakness …"
>
> 34:3-4

☙

SAINT BENEDICT DOES not want his sons or daughters to misinterpret the passage from the Acts of the Apostles (Acts 4:35) about distribution according to need. What is need? How are needs different from wants? A wise person once said that if your wants are something you think you need, then you are a slave. If only your *real* needs are your wants, then you are truly free. A need is something you cannot live without, whereas a want is something you don't want to live without. You need rest; but if you sleep more than eight hours a day, perhaps you are overindulging and subject to the demon of sloth.

In further reflection, Saint Benedict reminds the sick that they are a blessing for their brothers and sisters and that this truth should be their great comfort. The infirm are "saint-makers" for those who show them constant mercy and healing love. Taking care of someone who cannot take care of himself is a fulfillment of the command of the Lord Jesus, "Whatever you do to the least of My brothers, that you do unto Me" (Mt 25:40).

Finally, our holy Father Benedict addresses the evil of murmuring. Knowing full well how destructive murmuring can be from his own experience of life in community, he warns his children in Christ that it's all too easy to whisper a complaint about the need to care for others' needs. Indeed, this is the worst vice found in monasteries because it destroys the morale of the monks. It is a vice that grows out of the failure that is a lack of faith. The monk or nun who chooses to be unable to see Christ in needy people is refusing to worship Him through loving service to His "least ones." Indeed, this attitude echoes the fallen angel Lucifer's "*Non serviam*" ("I will not serve").

Fr. Andrew Campbell, O.S.B.

CHAPTER 34
1-7

"In this way all the members will be at peace."

34:5

※

"That's not fair!" Children are keenly aware when toys or desserts are not distributed equally. "Sister got an ice cream cone with two scoops, and I got only one – not fair!" "Davey had his turn at show-and-tell, and I want my turn <u>now</u>!" Does that sound familiar?

Parents and teachers understand fairness differently. The equal distribution of food, time slots, or material items is not always genuinely "fair," and it may not even be possible. Saint Benedict knew that equal distribution is not ideal for those in greater need or those in lesser need. Providing a greater or smaller amount for each monk's needs is not only prudent but is also critical for the survival of a monastic community.

Although practical stewardship of the material goods of the monastery, which Saint Benedict compares to "sacred vessels of the altar" (*RB* 31:10), is undisputable, his concerns go beyond the material. He is deeply concerned for the spiritual as well as the corporal, for souls as well as bodies. Monks who are ill need more care, whereas the healthy should be grateful that such care is given and offer thanks to God for being well. This attitude of gratitude enables monks to see the hand of God in everything and thus to advance in the "school of the Lord's service." In conjunction with nurturing gratitude and humility, Benedict warns all monks to beware of grumbling, the infectious attitude that corrodes the very spiritual foundations of the monastic community.

The faith of the good monk brings him joy, for he knows that he is taken care of by God through the abbot and the community. All the more does the practice of simplicity add to his joy because he is freed from greed, hoarding, and all that could distract him from his primary Christian goal: to seek God above all else. The straight and narrow path is simple but not easy; it is, however, the absolutely necessary way to everlasting life.

Fr. Alfred Patterson, O.S.B.

CHAPTER 35
1-11

"The brothers should serve one another."

35:1

☙

AT FIRST GLANCE, we might be tempted to ask why Saint Benedict would spend so much time describing the menial tasks of the monastery. Perhaps there is something more to this passage than simply the identification of who washes the dirty towels at the end of the week. In these eleven short verses, some form of the word *service* appears eight times in the English translation. While the word appears here in the context of kitchen serving, service in general is an important theme in the *Rule* and in the Gospels. Every day we are called to live a life of service to our brothers and sisters, to live out Gospel values in even the smallest things we do.

Sometimes we think and act as if we could earn salvation in one or two heroic acts of virtue. Saint Benedict shows us in this chapter that our salvation is worked out gradually in everyday life and everyday decisions. Our witness to faith is not necessarily a dramatic martyrdom or a call to sacrifice everything at once; rather this witness happens more often in the simple giving of a cup of cold water to one of God's little ones (cf. Mt 10:42, Mk 9:41).

BR. MICHAEL ANTONACCI, O.S.B.

CHAPTER 35
12-18

"God, come to my assistance;
Lord, make haste to help me (Ps 69[70]:2)."

35:17

༄

SAINT BENEDICT UNDERSTOOD that those who cook and serve daily meals to monks, as in any family, must begin and end their tasks with prayer if the work given to them by God is to go well. First, however, the admonition is given that they should receive extra drink and bread. Thus we enter again into the great mystery that in breaking bread together not only are our bodies fed but our souls are nourished as well.

According to our modern custom of eating, three times a day there are opportunities to give to others as gift the work of hand and heart. No doubt, the effort requires discipline and perseverance in the face of culinary failure, and it requires humility when all goes well. Hence, the giving of extra portions to the workers so that they may serve "without grumbling or hardship" (35:13). Attitude, it turns out, is everything, especially in cooking!

Great cooks understand the importance of all the virtues being placed at the disposal of their art. Beautiful meals require planning, preparation, patience, tenderness, and creativity. It is love made visible and offered in faith for the pleasure and care of those who come hungry to the table.

"Blessed are you, Lord God, who have helped me and comforted me" (35:16; Ps 86:17).

CLAUDIA KNOWLTON

CHAPTER 36
1-10

"Care of the sick must rank above and before all else, so that they may be truly served as Christ …"

36:1

୧୨

AFTER THE FIRST verse of this chapter, Saint Benedict quotes the famous passage from Saint Matthew's Gospel on the Last Judgment: "'I was sick, and you visited me,' and, 'What you did for one of these least brothers you did for me'" (36:2, 3; Mt 25:36, 40). Now that I am retired and living in our infirmary (sometimes called the "sick floor"), I can understand how important are these words as I daily see and visit "these least brothers," eat with them, and celebrate Mass for them. I have known some of them for a long time and remember when they were younger and vigorous in their ministries as writers, teachers, and pastors. Now some can walk only with walkers or are in wheelchairs. The years have caused some to lose their short-term or long-term memories. Still, the gleam in their eyes reminds me of their more active past years. In many cases, these senior monks *are* our oral history as story-tellers of events from years ago in the monastery. They form a very rich treasure. We must appreciate them and recognize the blessing of being with them.

FR. WILLIAM A. BEAVER, O.S.B.

CHAPTER 36
1-10

> "The abbot must take the greatest care that ... those who serve the sick do not neglect them ..."
>
> 36:10

❧

THIS CHAPTER BEGINS, "Care of the sick must rank above and before all else ..." (36:1). As Oblates who form an extension of the Benedictine community, we pray for "freedom from distress," although that freedom does not come naturally. Each person whom we meet suffers loss and experiences pain, aging, or diminishment of life or of relationships, each in his or her own way. Each one feels pangs of disappointment, of doubt, and of difficulty in making certain decisions. These are all "dis-ease." Can we, as Christians, provide them with necessary space, compassion, and time to heal, not as an indulgence but with heartfelt care, with active, attentive listening, and with charitable service? Neglect and indifference dishonor our sick brothers and sisters.

Furthermore, we might ask the questions, "Who is my brother? Who is my sister?" Christ's mercy and compassion are prevalent in the miracles of His ministry. As Oblates, we must answer to our consciences as we encounter pleas for help, both those that are uttered and those that are silent. How do we witness to our faith? Do we strive to see Christ in all whom we meet? We must be open to opportunities to serve. We must also be willing to reflect on our own successes and failures in charity and humility, with the intention of growing in eagerness to grant a Christ-like response to others in need.

Richard H. Fitzgerald

CHAPTER 37
1-3

"[The old and the young] should be treated with kindly consideration and allowed to eat before the regular hours."

37:3

☙

IN THE PRESCRIPTIONS of the *Rule*, Saint Benedict intended to be firm but also to show compassion and not to impose undue burdens. The primary purpose of Chapter 37, like Chapter 39, was to ensure that food be provided to the community in sufficient quantity and for adequate nourishment. Since most monks were engaged in manual labor, it was vital that they maintained good physical health. However, the monastery also included elderly and infirm monks as well as "boy Oblates." For these groups Saint Benedict made exceptions to the standard regulations.

As Oblates, we should be kind, compassionate, considerate, and patient with the vulnerable groups of our society, in particular the young and the old. Fortunately, in our contemporary society we have made great strides in caring for people, especially the elderly. People are living longer, and many of us are faced with being caregivers for elderly parents and relatives. Giving such care for those suffering from dementia and Alzheimer's disease can be especially difficult. Civil authorities have also progressed in recognizing the needs of the elderly, as with handicap parking permits and sloped pavements at crosswalks.

In sum, Chapter 37 is very relevant today. It reminds us to be grateful for advances in health care and in consideration for vulnerable people. It also challenges us to recognize where our society is deficient and to discern how we might show more personal concern for the aged and for youth, especially those who are not given the personal loving care that God would want them to have.

JOSEPH C. CIRELLI

CHAPTER 38
1-12

> "The brothers should by turn serve one another's needs as they eat and drink, so that no one need ask for anything."
>
> 38:6

༄

THIS CHAPTER GIVES us an insight into some of the day-to-day realities of the monastery that Saint Benedict envisioned. Taking note of what could be beneficial for us today, I would like to focus in particular on verses 6 and 7. These verses make it explicit that, even while eating, the monk is to be conscientious in his awareness of and responsiveness to the needs of others. However, he is also to maintain readiness for a word that might come from the Lord and the benefit potentially brought about by attentiveness to the reading done at the meal, a benefit that speaking would hinder. It is impressive that these verses indicate that Benedict hoped the monks would be so attentive to others that no sort of communication would be needed at all! Similar consideration for others is found in verses 10 and 12. Although each of these verses deals with a different aspect of "The Reader for the Week," together they give us a glimpse of the kind of charity and consideration that was to be the standard and guide in even relatively minor, day-to-day procedures of the monastery. They offer a reminder that charity is the goal and purpose of the Christian life, to say nothing of the monastic life.

BR. MATTHEW LAMBERT, O.S.B.

CHAPTER 39
1-11

" ... and if fruit or fresh vegetables are available, a third dish may also be added."

39:3

☙

THE OVERALL MONASTIC regime set forth by Saint Benedict is a moderate one, and his legislation on the proper amount of food and drink is no exception. Saint Benedict warns about overindulgence at the end of the chapter, which he says is inconsistent with the life of a Christian. However, as a loving father to his community, he prescribes a regimen for meals that gives his monks the energy to perform their labors and the contentment that will keep them from murmuring. The provision for a variety of cooked dishes, for fruit and fresh vegetables (when in season), and for a large allotment of bread indicates that Saint Benedict wants the monastic fare to be both nourishing and enjoyable.

Eating is a necessity, but Saint Benedict seems to try to make this necessary process one of grace and charity. Wishing to satisfy his monks, Saint Benedict allows them to select temperately from the prepared dishes. Benedictine monastic communities eat their meals together. Coming together to dine not only sustains them physically for the duties of the day but also cultivates a spirit of thanksgiving and unity. Grace-filled eating also prepares people for divine communion now and in the age to come. Let us strive to make meal times in families and communities opportunities to grow in holiness.

JOSEPH DUCHENE

CHAPTER 40
1-9

"[The superior] must, in any case, take great care lest excess or drunkenness creep in."

40:5

☙

SAINT BENEDICT ACKNOWLEDGES the delicate nature of specifying the amount of food and drink consumed by others (40:2). He also recognizes that God gives each of us different gifts (cf. 1 Cor 7:7). It is with these considerations that the *Rule* states that a half-bottle of wine a day should be sufficient drink for an individual.

Saint Benedict also warns that a monk must guard against drinking to excess. The temptation not to be sober is one of the snares set by Satan, and there are two prime examples in the Old Testament. Noah's drunkenness (Gen 9:20-27) led to his son Ham's sinning and then to a curse put upon Canaan, Ham's son. A second example involves Lot's daughters' enticing their father to drink and then having relations with him to preserve their family line (Gen 19:30-38). As a consequence their sons, Ammon and Moab, became great nations that were enemies of Israel.

The apostle Paul also shows us the way to moderation. In his Letter to the Philippians he says that in every circumstance he has learned to be content (Phil 4:11-12). He strives to bless God at all times and to put the love of Christ first in his life; this theme is echoed by the *Rule*'s stating that the monk should "bless God and not grumble" (40:8).

Verse 40:8 has helped me very much personally. Circumstances in my life dictated that some responsibilities be taken away from me at my parish; in particular, I was no longer allowed to serve as lector at Mass, though that was a role that I loved. Instead of dwelling on the deprivation with a negative attitude, I realized that God had to be glorified in this situation. I also knew that He had other plans for me – e.g., to spread His word in other ways. These realizations brought me hope when I was in a valley of despair and kept me from being dominated by pride.

In conclusion, the key to this chapter of the *Rule* is the virtue of temperance. Drink must never become an idol in our lives. We can practice temperance to glorify God and, at the same time, learn to be gracious givers to those in need. Thus we can avoid the wiles of Satan and display true charity.

Louis Jacobs

CHAPTER 41
1-9

"Similarly, [the abbot] should so regulate and arrange all matters that souls may be saved ..."

41:5

☙

SAINT BENEDICT IS practical about everything in his "little rule." It is not surprising that there is even a chapter specifying when the monks are to take their meals. At first glance there does not seem to be any spiritual nourishment in these verses; they seem only to describe another detail about the monastic life. Even when I looked at a few commentaries, they just explained the calendar of Saint Benedict's time. Yet there is one line that is especially worth pondering: "[the abbot] should so regulate and arrange all matters that souls may be saved and the brothers may go about their activities without justifiable grumbling" (41:5).

It is easy to become anxious about our needs in this world; our culture seems to dictate that we always be planning for the next event and thus never be content with what we have or with where we are now. In strictly regulating the times for meals, Saint Benedict is showing us that although we do not control everything, such lack of control should not be a cause for worry. It can, on the contrary, hasten us on the way of salvation. When we truly acknowledge that God is in control, we can give up trying to rule this world. Letting go of the reins of control can help us to look forward to taking part in the life of the next world.

BR. JOACHIM MORGAN, O.S.B.

CHAPTER 42
1-11

"Monks should diligently cultivate silence at all times, but especially at night."

42:1

❧

EVERY DAY THERE are some special times in everyone's life; bodily necessity demands at least both food and sleep. In other chapters, Saint Benedict discusses how we can arrange our eating so that it can work against vices and draw us closer to God. In this chapter, Saint Benedict offers us valuable wisdom about how to arrange that special time of the day that comes before the night's rest. There are four notable aspects of Saint Benedict's daily preparation for sleep: gathering together, reading, prayer, and silence. The effect of this preparation is to draw the monk out of himself into communion with God before entering into the night's rest. Sleep, as a merely bodily exercise, is an inherently selfish activity insofar as we always sleep alone. (Even when our bodies are physically with someone else, the unconsciousness of sleep brings us into ourselves and away from everyone.) As a result, unless we are spiritually moving out of ourselves as we prepare for sleep, it could magnify other selfish habits and selfish ways of thinking. Saint Benedict spiritually facilitates our moving out of ourselves by bringing the monks together before bed. Then he calls for focused attention outside of themselves as the monks listen, together, to an edifying spiritual text. It is not meant to be a difficult text (like the Heptateuch) but a simpler, more enjoyable one like the *Conferences* of Cassian or the *Lives of the Saints*. Such a text would also become comfortably familiar over the course of many years. The final step of drawing the monk spiritually outside of himself is through the praying of Compline, together with the other monks. At that point, Saint Benedict enforces silence in order to leave the monk, drawn out of himself, in loving union with God as he enters into the night's rest.

>Fr. Boniface Hicks, O.S.B.

CHAPTER 43
1-12

"Indeed, nothing is to be preferred to the Work of God."

43:3

☙

THE "SIGNAL" FOR the Work of God is the bell, understood as the "Vox Dei," the voice of God calling to pray. By stopping whatever we are doing at the moment and "hastening with great speed," we are fulfilling Benedict's admonition that "nothing be put before the Work of God." There is always the temptation to squeeze out a few more minutes of work before leaving for prayer and thus to risk arriving just as prayer begins; such a response implies that we had more important things to attend to than to go to prayer. What is worse is arriving after prayer has begun. Benedict has harsh words for those who arrive late. They are to stand out of their usual place so that they will suffer the embarrassment of being seen by all. It may seem like a small matter, but it is a matter of priorities. When understood in the greater context of faith, arriving late is actually a sign of a lack of charity toward the community and of a lack of obedience to the voice of God. It is God who continually calls us away from our selfish interests and back to our "First Love."

What are our priorities? In what other ways is the voice of God calling us from concern for self to an emptying of self, because of love for God and for others, in the ordinary course of each day?

FR. VINCENT DE PAUL CROSBY, O.S.B.

CHAPTER 43
13-19

"No one is to presume to eat or drink before or after the time appointed."

43:18

☙

REGARDING COMING LATE to the Divine Office or a meal, Saint Benedict is very transparent. The sanctions apply only if this failure happens through the monk's own negligence or fault. The degree of personal responsibility must be considered in the matter of all apparent faults. Similar situations can occur today. Sanctions can be applied without a careful look at the underlying reality. That is to say, no sanction should be imposed at all if a brother comes late and it is not his fault. The same applies if a brother misses the Divine Office altogether.

Monks are human and, like everyone else, have good and bad habits, virtues and vices. The cultivation of good habits in the monastery helps us to abide fully in the present moment and to live a committed monastic life that is both strong and fruitful. What looks like a virtue might be only a habit that we have learned. If we lose the inner spiritual meaning of what we are doing, we may end up losing contact with God in certain areas of our lives.

At the end of this chapter, there is a caution against eating outside the normal, scheduled eating times. This vice is a major problem in our modern culture. Many people grew up eating when they felt like it and thus may have little or no discipline regarding food. In such a situation it is difficult to recapture the value of a communal meal.

In the last verse, Saint Benedict describes what must have been a normal situation in his time, namely the offering of something good to a monk, who then turns it down. After that experience, Saint Benedict says, he must not ask for it again. This regulation calls upon the monk to humble himself for being so indecisive.

The teaching in this chapter for our spiritual well-being is clear; we are to live with conviction, strength, and vigor the vocation to which we have been called. If we have committed a fault, we are humbly to accept the penance. If we have not been responsible for an irregularity, then we should not be blamed. From this passage it is also evident that the monk, Oblate, and every Christian are called to holiness, a holiness that means being whole and authentic. As Saint Irenaeus puts it, we are called to "be fully alive in Christ"!

Fr. Chad Ficorilli, O.S.B.

CHAPTER 44
1-10

"Those excommunicated for less serious faults from the table only are to make satisfaction in the oratory for as long as the abbot orders."

44:9

☙

THIS CHAPTER CONCERNS a phenomenon called "satisfaction." According to Appendix 4, section d) of the expanded version of *RB 1980* (page 435), "[satisfaction] is the procedure whereby one acknowledges a fault (*RB* 7:44) and carries out the imposed penalties (*RB* 43:12; 44; 46:3; 71:8). ... It is a concrete and, as it were, 'sacramental' procedure that should normally repair damaged relationships and eradicate pride in the offender." I encourage you to read this whole section. By making satisfaction the offender is "regaining one's right relationship with God."

How do we begin to make satisfaction? We do so by opening our hearts to God and relying on His strength. Our Blessed Virgin Mary gives us five "little stones" as weapons against our "Goliaths":

1. Pray the rosary with an open heart.
2. Receive the Eucharist regularly; this sacrament is your food.
3. Read the Holy Bible, and listen with an open heart.
4. Fast on bread and water every Wednesday and Friday, if you can, for our Blessed Virgin Mary's intentions.
5. Go to confession monthly; this sacrament removes sin.

When we pray the rosary, we can invoke the Holy Spirit and recognize that the mysteries we pray and most of the words themselves are part of God's revelation.

DEBORAH JOHNSTON

CHAPTER 45
1-3

"If he does not use this occasion to humble himself, he will be subjected to more severe punishment …"

45:1

☙

Our culture, except possibly in the business world, tends to be lax about mistakes. It may be a good thing that we are not harsh with people who make mistakes in speaking or writing since by its very definition a "mistake" is unintended and may be grounded in ignorance. However, mistakes do have consequences, and sometimes very serious ones. If teachers never correct a pupil's errors in math or grammar, the pupil will grow up deficient in his mathematical or communication skills. The effects of having error-prone people as mechanics, teachers, lawyers, or doctors could be extremely damaging or even fatal.

Saint Benedict says that those who make mistakes in choir should apologize publicly right away. The correction will be beneficial for the community and beneficial for the erring monk's growth in humility. The "more severe punishment" given to the monk who fails to accept correction is meant to help him to overcome pride and to be more mindful of the effects of his mistakes. One must learn that it is a matter of charity to try to avoid mistakes!

Our mistakes can become grace-filled opportunities for growth if we admit quickly, at least to ourselves, that we have been in error. When others are directly involved, it is important to apologize promptly. We grow in humility by acknowledging our frailty. We grow in trust by realizing that we cannot succeed or improve without God's grace. Furthermore, if the "mistakes" are actually sins, then we can benefit by opening ourselves to the floodgates of God's mercy. For those of us who are Catholic, we have the great blessing of frequent recourse to the Sacrament of Reconciliation to receive mercy and forgiveness and thus to become more merciful in dealing with others who sin against us – or whose mistakes cause us frustration.

Fr. Donald Raila, O.S.B.

CHAPTER 46
1-6

"[They] know how to heal their own wounds as well as those of others …"

46:6

❧

As we see in other chapters of the *Rule*, here we once again learn of Saint Benedict's concern for the healing of spiritual wounds and for progress toward holiness. The committing of public faults requires a public apology and a public satisfaction. Prompt acknowledgment is a healthy policy for the individual and the community. It nurtures responsibility, humility, and ownership of one's actions, even of accidental failings. This sense of ownership of faults goes against the current trend of jumping into blame of others for all one's miseries.

On a deeper level, a monk's hidden sins are to be revealed only to the abbot or a spiritual elder, one who is seasoned in healing wounds and keeping confidences. Seeking spiritual direction and confessing one's sins are two different (though related) practices, but both are important for every monk, given the seriousness of our calling to seek God intently and to grow in our relationship with Him. There is no growth without the pain of acknowledging one's sins and the determination to implore God for His mercy.

There is a two-fold message here for Christians who live outside the monastery. One is that we all need someone to whom we can reveal our faults and sins. Unfortunately, there are not enough spiritual directors to accommodate everyone who wants a director. Still, a Christian should be able to find a friend or family member with whom he can share his innermost thoughts and feelings and from whom he can receive spiritual guidance.

A second message is for those who serve as "spiritual elders" and help to heal the wounds of others. Whether we are a spiritual director or a friend of someone who approaches us for spiritual healing, we need to ask for the grace to listen well, to be compassionate, and to take seriously the implicit or explicit pledge never to reveal to others what is spoken in confidence. (Of course, this commitment is most urgent for priests administering the Sacrament of Penance.) When we help to guide others spiritually in cooperation with the Holy Spirit, we are doing the very work of Christ Himself, the Divine Physician. Let us be in awe of this great responsibility.

Fr. Donald Raila, O.S.B.

CHAPTER 47
1-4

"It is the abbot's care to announce, day and night, the hour for the Work of God."

47:1

☙

Today a simple alarm clock could take care of the job of alerting the community about the next event in a monastic schedule. It was a little more complicated in Saint Benedict's era. The abbot had to be attentive to the flux of season and the shadow on the sundial. Once one had lived in a monastery for a few years, the rhythm of prayer should have become encoded in one's body, which would be ready to rise at the proper time and be moved to gather with other monks every few hours to join in the divine praises. By the time one was elected abbot, he would have become an expert at such interior calculations. Such a responsibility is a symbol of the whole loving service demanded of the abbot, even today. He is to be careful to summon the brethren to prayer, chapter meetings, meals, and work; indeed, it is the abbot's responsibility to make sure that everything is done at the proper time.

The peaceful flow of life within the soul and among the monks creates a mutual interdependence, which is the intention of the *Holy Rule*. Even such simple tasks as intoning the antiphons or reading in the chapel or in the refectory are not left up to the random selection, say, of the monk who arrives first. Only those who edify the hearers are chosen. We all need inspiration when we gather for the Divine Office or for meals; we all need to be summoned by the Holy Spirit back into prayer so that we can be tolerant of one another's weaknesses, which often reveal themselves in choir or at meals. Only someone who is humble, serious, and reverent will be able to participate in the abbot's care of the community. Without humility, one cannot proclaim the Word of God; the reader will think that it's "all about him" and his talent. Without gravity or seriousness, one cannot proclaim the Word of God; the reader will think that it's all about how easily he can get a chuckle out of the brethren. Without reverence, one cannot proclaim the Word of God; the reader will think it's all about others' noticing how humble he is in the performance of his duty.

Fr. Andrew Campbell, O.S.B.

CHAPTER 48
1-9

"... the brothers should have specified periods for manual labor as well as for prayerful reading."

48:1

☙

WHILE VACATIONERS ATTEMPTED to anchor blankets and to secure small items in the midst of constant wind gusts on the shore, a small, bright-yellow butterfly steadily persisted in a seemingly impossible balancing act. In spite of the threat held within each movement of the wind, the swerving butterfly mastered its flight to advance until it was no longer seen on the beach. When I shared this experience with my husband, he remarked that through the eyes of an engineer the butterfly has exactly the right balance of strength and flexibility to fly successfully in gusty winds. If either strength or flexibility were in excess, the butterfly would be overburdened.

This experience seems to capture the heart of the first verses of Chapter 48, which warns against idleness and highlights the importance of balance among work, study, and prayer through the mandating of specific time periods for each. This legislation is moderated to suit each monk while it remains responsive to the community's needs of the day. Strength and flexibility balance each other so that no monk is excessively burdened or insufficiently challenged. This consideration nurtures health in mind, body, and soul and frees the monk to "prefer Christ above all else" (cf. 72:11) so that "in all things God may be glorified" (57:9).

There are times when life's "wind gusts" threaten to disrupt the necessary and delicate balance of work, study, and prayer. If self-discipline is neglected during those times, strength and flexibility suffer so that the soul cannot listen fully in prayer and cannot act charitably in community. Personal activity becomes separated from God's will, and this loss of integration creates a void in the soul that opens the door to temptations. This situation can lead to further disorder, in which extremes may overpower and lethargy may predominate. By rejecting the discipline of the *Rule*, a soul can place itself at a precarious distance from the community and from God. With self-discipline motivated by the grace of God, the soul may return to a balanced state in which God is served. This restoration of health can be assisted by a prayerful reading of the *Rule* and a determined living of the *Rule*.

The butterfly is one of God's magnificent creations. Though very delicate, it is engineered to fly in the midst of seemingly impossible wind currents. Fragile man is likewise created with a soul capable of enduring great trials and progressing amid seemingly impossible challenges. The butterfly's life begins as a lowly caterpillar, and then through metamorphosis it fulfills its final purpose. By God's grace man becomes capable of similar transformation from a base creature to a fully mature human person who radiates the love and goodness of God. This transformation is possible through Christ, with the additional help of a disciplined acceptance of the *Rule*, which is "engineered" to be completely compatible with our human nature.

Mary Ann Kaufman

CHAPTER 48
10-21

> "[The supervising seniors'] duty is to see that no brother is so apathetic as to waste time or engage in idle talk …"
>
> 48:18

☙

BLESSED (and soon-to-be Saint) John Paul II wrote of Saint Benedict, "Let us listen to St. Benedict's voice; from interior solitude, from contemplative silence, from victory over the noise of the outer world …" (P.J. Paul, *Prayers and Devotions from Pope John Paul II* (New York: Penguin Books, 1988), page 254).

How many hours a day do we spend watching television, reading the newspaper, or searching the Internet? Imagine if we devoted half of the time spent on these activities to reading the Bible, practicing *lectio divina*, or praying the Divine Office! The monks of the sixth century did not have distractions from electronic devices or newspapers; yet the *Rule* reminds us of the deadly sin of sloth. Saint Benedict remarks starkly, "Idleness is the enemy of the soul" (48:1).

At Terce (about 9:00 A.M.), Sext (about 12:00 P.M.), and None (about 3:00 P.M.), the monks paused for the "Little Hours." During our work day it is important to pause now and then to ask God for assistance in the work we are doing and to make sure that we are doing it for Him. Lunch time is an ideal time to pray the Divine Office or to read some Scripture. During Lent we might consider fasting and so spend lunch time and breaks reading or praying. Furthermore, silence can be beautiful "music," like a symphony within the soul. The voice of God can be heard more clearly in the quiet atmosphere behind a closed door and within an open heart. The monk or follower of the *Rule* is cautioned not to waste time. The spiritual and practical application is to think about each day as an opportunity to serve God, both in our work and in our prayer. We might ask ourselves, "How do I spend my time? How much time is devoted to work, family, spiritual reading, and prayer? Are these dimensions well balanced in my life?" The clock is ticking, and we can never regain those minutes wasted; so let us use well the minutes that are coming to us!

Edward Rezek

CHAPTER 48
22-25

"On Sunday all are to be engaged in reading …"

48:22

☙

IN THE JEWISH tradition the Sabbath is a day of rest and renewal, an opportunity to spend time in prayer and in study of the Sacred Scriptures. Such a weekly practice helps to guarantee respect for human dignity as well as to provide refreshment and proper nourishment for the human person. We do not need to look far to see that our contemporary Western society treats human beings more like machines than creatures with God-given dignity. Some phenomena that give evidence of this degradation are jobs requiring rotating shifts, the progressive shrinking of vacation times, "emergency calls" at home that require a worker to return to work to repair something, and the trend of going to work extra hours on weekends in order to "catch up." Our tendency to workaholism masks itself as dedication, hard work, and reliability; meanwhile, we actually suffer under a modern form of slavery.

Saint Benedict wisely demands that everyone in the community engage in "prayerful reading" (48:1) on Sundays. No one can work all day, every day. Human beings need rest and spiritual as well as intellectual nourishment in order to lead happy, healthy lives. Having a little bit of this freedom each day, as well as on one full day of the week, is an authentic practice of leisure. Without genuine leisure, there is no space for creativity, re-creation, or any other genuinely human activity.

BR. MICHAEL ANTONACCI, O.S.B.

CHAPTER 49
1-10

> "so that each of us will have something above the assigned measure to offer God of his own will *with the joy of the Holy Spirit* (1 Thes 1:6)."
>
> 49:6

❧

SAINT BENEDICT BEGINS Chapter 49 by stating that the life of a monk ought always to have about it the character of a Lenten observance. True as this is, I suspect that most people would gasp at the thought that the whole of their lives need to be characterized by Lenten disciplines; they would be likely to pass over this statement and move on, with the hope that somehow this prescription does not really apply. The asceticism of Lent can be challenging enough to practice during Lent without considering it for the rest of the year.

I would like to propose another way of looking at Saint Benedict's admonition. While it is important to engage in the practices of our Lenten observance, how we engage in them is also worth considering. In *RB* 49:6, Saint Benedict says that we should offer something extra to God "with the joy of the Holy Spirit" (1 Thes 1:6). Then again in 49:7, he specifies that we should await Holy Easter with the joy of spiritual desire.

Thus the practices of Lent and the year-round practices of monastic life are gateways to joy, a joy that can be found in no other way. Restraining ourselves from vices, giving ourselves over to asceticism, praying intensely, and engaging in holy reading (*lectio divina*) are the ways of entering into joy and not obstacles to joy. It is a joy that obliges us, if we are true to the way of Saint Benedict, at all times. Do we have the courage to be joyful at all times?

Fr. Kurt Belsole, O.S.B.

CHAPTER 50
1–4

"Brothers who work so far away that they cannot return to the oratory at the proper time ... are to perform the Work of God where they are ..."

50:1, 3

☙

IN THE DISTANT reaches of a vineyard, the glistening dew of dawn calls a brother to prayer. He removes his sandals, and kneeling on the ground of the earth, he reminds himself of his far-off brethren and chants in unity with them, "Lord, open my lips, and my mouth will declare your praise." The inner radiance of God's creation once again blooms to meet the red glow of the sun that opened it. Immersed in the sweet fragrance of that joy, the morning praise of the brother and of his brethren at other locations merges with the mist of the field as it rises toward the heavens.

Likewise, in the heat of high noon, a brother allows his body a break from his manual labor. He kneels in the shadow of the lush, green vine leaves around him and the rich, dark soil beneath him and recalls that he, too, is part of creation. He longs to be with his brethren but finds peace in knowing that his abbot has directed him to this corner of a field, and that his founder has instructed him to pray where he finds himself at the prescribed hour. Therefore, he recites psalms from memory, and when his prayers are finished, he nourishes his body with the fruit that surrounds him.

Weary from the labors of the day, a brother welcomes the coolness of dusk as does the land that he has been tending.

The blossoms close their petals to the pastel colors of the sky while the monk lifts his hood to shield his head from the dewfall. Kneeling under the faint glimmer of the brightest stars and amongst the intermittent glows of the fireflies, he bows his head in thanksgiving saying, "O God, come to my assistance; O Lord, make haste to help me." His soul gradually enters into silent communion with his brethren at the monastery and with creation as his spirit begins to rest in the stillness of the Divine.

After a day of prayer and work, the music of the crickets accompanies his steady pace as he returns to the abbey. At supper he breaks bread with his brethren. They too have been working in the fields, each in accord with his talents, and he delights in the stories they tell and that he tells them. Their hearts are gladdened in the common bond they share with one another and with Christ, strengthened especially by their having prayed of the Work of God.

Vincent Thomas

CHAPTER 51
1-3

"[The brother] must not presume to eat outside, even if he receives a pressing invitation."

51:1

❦

THIS CHAPTER ADDRESSES the issue of meals for monks who are on a short journey. Saint Benedict indicates that the monks are to avoid eating even when they are invited, unless the abbot has given permission. The reasons that have been cited by Benedictine writers focus on the goal of maintaining monastic practice, with the understanding that meals taken outside the monastery conflict with this goal.

Monastic practices include common prayer and *lectio divina,* which form and maintain the interior spiritual life according to the Word of God. Continual recollection is essential for this focus on God and His word, and it is necessary to minimize distractions. In contrast, a journey inevitably involves distractions, and so when a monk has to travel, these should be avoided or minimized. A meal that is in keeping with monastic practice is both prayerful and reflective. In contrast, a meal in a secular or public environment does not foster prayer and reflection and, therefore, does not support the interior spiritual life. Instead of taking a meal on a journey, one might better use the time for prayer and reflection. This strategy serves not only to avoid eating in a problematic environment, but also enables the journey to contribute to one's interior spiritual life rather than to detract from it.

BR. HUGH LESTER, O.S.B.

CHAPTER 52
1-5

*"The oratory ought to be what it is called,
and nothing else is to be done or stored there."*

52:1

☙

OUR FATHER SAINT Benedict is aware of the importance of having a unique place dedicated to the praise of God, namely the oratory of the monastery. It is the place where the Divine Office and other liturgies are celebrated. The environment of the oratory fosters listening to the voice of God, keeping one's heart open to God with interior silence, and praying with heartfelt devotion. Having such a place might enable every Christian to have a personal encounter with God. There the community praises God and gives thanks to Him with one heart and one voice. The oratory has no other purpose than to help the monk to seek an encounter with God. There should be no room for any sort of distractions, such as secular objects or noisy thoughts. For the human beings who pray there, the one thing necessary is that their intellects and wills be in accord with God's love and will. This sacred and holy place is a space where His Word and Spirit are present in a special way and where the two dimensions of the kingdom of God, one earthly and one heavenly, join each other. We truly believe: "How lovely is your dwelling place, O Lord of hosts … Blessed are those who dwell in your house, forever singing your praise!" (Ps. 84:1, 4).

BR. MARTINHO ZEVALLOS, O.S.B.

CHAPTER 53
1-15

"All guests who present themselves are to be welcomed as Christ …"

53:1

☙

I OFTEN WONDER whether, when Benedict was writing these verses of his *Rule*, he was remembering the famous passage of Genesis 18:1-5, in which God sent three men to visit Abraham about the coming birth of Isaac. The Scripture says that Abraham "ran from the entrance of the tent to greet them; and bowing to the ground" (18:2), he offered to bathe their feet and refresh them with a meal. Then, with Sarah's help, he prepared a fine dinner to nourish them. For the Jews high standards of hospitality were an important part of their moral code; they saw such lavish treatment of guests as a response to God. And then what a surprise Sarah had!

Benedict tells us that guests must be welcomed as Christ (v. 1). This mode of hospitality has become a hallmark of Benedictines, whether they reside in the monastery or in some mission on the outside. They strive to regard each visitor as a reflection of Jesus Himself. The bow is meant to acknowledge the presence of Christ in the other. One might also recall the experience of Saint Francis at the time of his conversion. At first, while on his walks, he avoided a leper as an undesirable stranger; but then he finally went over to embrace him since he learned that the "stranger" was actually Christ in disguise.

FR. WILLIAM A. BEAVER, O.S.B.

CHAPTER 53
16-24

> "The kitchen for the abbot and guests ought to be separate, so that guests—and monasteries are never without them—need not disturb the brothers when they present themselves at unpredictable hours."
>
> 53:16

☙

It is good to speak about verse 16 bluntly and say that the notion of having an abbot eat apart from the community has never worked. The abbot should not, on a regular basis, absent himself from the refectory where the rest of the monks eat. The *Holy Rule* presupposes that the abbot will eat with the guests when it is appropriate and that if there are no guests, he will invite some monks to eat with him. Such separation from the monastic community does not work out well.

It is still important that the abbot actually have some interaction with guests. Here at Saint Vincent, the archabbot regularly interacts with guests as occasions arise while he does not necessarily eat with them. Because of the abbot's administrative responsibilities and the need to be present to the monks of the monastery, fulfilling the function of interacting with guests can be difficult. It is the specific duty of the guest master and his assistants to offer hospitality to guests when they arrive. It is also important that the care and upkeep of the guest rooms be entrusted to reliable assistants to the guest master as well as the guest master himself. Saint Benedict realizes that one person cannot do everything; so he provides for help wherever it is needed.

Saint Benedict's final provision in this chapter states that monks other than the guest master's crew were not to interact with guests on a regular basis. While most monks are expected to keep a healthy distance from guests, they may ask a guest for a blessing if, by chance, they happen to pass him by. This clear teaching of the *Rule* regarding monks and guests does have value today. Other than guests who are already friends of a particular monk, the monk should not go out of his way to develop a friendship with guests. This teaching is difficult to enforce. However, in order to preserve their vocations, monks need to persevere at refraining from over-involvement with guests, who need to know the monastic community primarily in the silence of the monastic setting. Let us be reminded of these truths as we pray that all of our guests be received as Christ and that we monks relate to them well even while we keep a certain distance.

Fr. Chad Ficorilli, O.S.B.

CHAPTER 54
1-5

"[A monk] must not presume to accept gifts sent him even by his parents without previously telling the abbot."

54:2

☙

When I read this section for the first time, I thought, "How cold this man Benedict was!" After some time and further prayerful musing, however, I started to see the wisdom behind these strict decrees. In the journey of my life thus far, I've had to be humbled before I was able to make a change. Being humbled was a motivator, if you will. I now realize that certain "things" that I had acquired over the years had only separated me from what was really important. Things <u>seen</u> can and will isolate me from the things <u>unseen</u> that I genuinely cherish and that will lead me to sanctification and perfection. Material things have always given me reason for envy, pride, greed, and selfishness. Even the possession of letters can be misconstrued and thus cause resentments or unrealistic expectations.

In my attachment to this world's goods, I was depending on people and things to make me happy instead of allowing God to fulfill His promises in my life. Things can distract me from both God's love for me and my love for God. As the Prologue of the *Rule* states, if there is strictness, the purpose is "to amend faults and to safeguard love" (Prol: 47). This is what obedience is all about. The final goal is to "prefer nothing whatever to Christ" (72:11). For these insights from the *Rule* I remain humbly grateful.

Christopher Brown

CHAPTER 55
1-14

"To provide for laundering and night wear, every monk will need two cowls and two tunics, but anything more must be taken away as superfluous."

55:10-11

☙

WHILE RECENTLY ONE of my teenage daughters and I were on a shopping trip for a special occasion, she insisted that she needed a new pair of black dress shoes. In response, I tried to compose my irritation and defuse the situation. All I could picture in my mind was her closet containing at least four pairs of differently styled black shoes.

This incident typifies a frequently occurring challenge in our materialistic twenty-first century, saturated by consumeristic attitudes and endless choices of styles, flavors, and varieties of nearly anything that we could desire. Chapter 55 of the *Rule* provides a reminder of Our Lord's concern for human beings' true bodily needs of adequate covering and protection from the elements along with His cautions about simplicity of life. Saint Benedict knew that such items as clothing and shoes often could become objects of worry, inordinate desire, vanity, or attachment, all of which derail a soul from its pursuit of holiness. He challenges us to quiet these impulses with a conscious plan of avoiding material excess and preventing the accumulation of unused, unneeded goods.

DONNA SUNSERI

CHAPTER 56
1-3

"... for the sake of maintaining discipline ..."

56:3

❧

THIS IS ONE of the shortest chapters of the *Rule*, and according to Dom Paul Delatte, O.S.B., there are varied interpretations. One big question is: if the abbot always eats with guests ("and monasteries are never without them" (53:16)), when will he ever eat with the other monks? Dom Paul points out that subsequent legislation required the abbot to eat primarily with his community and <u>not</u> with guests.

In any case, these few verses reflect Saint Benedict's desire for good order. Since the abbot is likely to be both a wise and a sociable man, it is he who, in addition to the guest master, can most effectively interact with guests. He may also ask some of the other monks to be at table with him for special reasons. (For example, one of the monks may be celebrating his ninety-fifth birthday, as has happened at St. Vincent.) On the other hand, when the abbot needs to be away, another senior monk should supervise the monks at meals.

What can these arrangements possibly mean for twenty-first century monks and Oblates? Most of us probably think that we do not need a superior to preside over our meals. We may even think that we can eat our meals whenever we wish, however we wish, and with whomever we wish. However, as Christians desiring ongoing growth, we do need to seek Christ always, even at meals, and we do need good order! Does not Saint Paul proclaim, "Whether you eat or drink – whatever you do – you should do all for the glory of God" (1 Cor 10:31)? Therefore, should we not pray grace with real gratitude and recollection? Should we not eat only what is truly healthful for us? Should we not speak only what is truly upbuilding and faith-enhancing? Should we not show heartfelt charity to our companions at table? Should we not avoid overindulgence, haste, and coarse language? For all these reasons it is surely important to have regularity at meals, to have a certain amount of self-discipline and expected order, and even to have someone presiding in order to keep the atmosphere charitable and Christ-centered. In any case, let us welcome Christ Himself to preside over our every meal!

These precepts may be especially applicable to the institution of family meals, which seems to be facing extinction in our culture. In the life of a family, regular meals together are extremely important. Next to praying together, eating together is crucial for a Christian family. If one parent needs to be away, it is prudent to have another responsible adult in charge of a meal so as to ensure regularity and good order. For Oblates and monks, we need to resist society's trend to minimize the importance of family meals. With good planning, the establishment of good family habits, and much mutual love, Christian families can make sure that the family meal, ideally occurring at least once a day, is maintained even when interruptions occur. Although families in the world cannot be expected to keep the regular schedule of monks, they can strive boldly, with the help of God's grace, not to allow outside activities, guests, or other intervening forces to damage a healthy regular discipline of praying, eating, and working together to build up and strengthen a truly Christian home, as it were a "little church."

Fr. Donald Raila, O.S.B.

CHAPTER 57
1-9

"If there are artisans in the monastery, they are to practice their craft with all humility, but only with the abbot's permission."

57:1

☙☙

IT IS CLEAR that our holy Father Benedict recognized the unique individuality of each monk and that he encouraged the monks to use their particular gifts for the common good. In the case of those who excelled as craftsmen or artists, he asked them to practice their crafts "with all humility" and only with the permission of the abbot. Artists and craftsmen can take something ordinary and transform it into something extraordinary. As a result, we tend to think of them as special. Benedict, however, would like us to understand that the artist is not a special kind of person but that each person is a special kind of artist. Thus the artist is not to see himself as "conferring [a benefit] on the monastery" (57:2), but like all the other monks he is simply offering his gifts for the common good.

What are the particular gifts that God has given us? Do we see them as a means of making a positive contribution to the community, and do we offer them freely and generously "so that in all things God may be glorified" (57:9; 1 Pt 4:11)?

FR. VINCENT DE PAUL CROSBY, O.S.B.

CHAPTER 58
1-16

"... if at the end of four or five days he has shown himself patient in bearing his harsh treatment and difficulty of entry ..."

58:3

༄

SAINT BENEDICT WAS never guilty of false advertisement; he never promised a rose garden to prospective members of his monastery. Great realist as he was, he wanted to make sure that each candidate for the novitiate would "be clearly told all the hardships and difficulties that will lead him to God" (58:8). If the prospective monk was truly seeking God rather than an easy life, then he would be eager "for the Work of God, for obedience, and for trials" (58:7). Trials and difficulties occur in every life, especially in lives dedicated explicitly to the following of Christ.

Instead of starry-eyed enthusiasm, Benedict expects perseverance in stability from a candidate. During his year of novitiate, the new monk will hear the whole *Rule* read to him three times, and each time he will be free to opt out. But if after all that he still stands firm, he may be received into the community as a vowed member. During Benedict's time, that one year of training and testing was the only period of preparation for a final commitment to monastic life. Since then, Canon Law has variously extended that time by introducing temporary vows (usually for a period of three years or more).

FR. SEBASTIAN SAMAY, O.S.B.

CHAPTER 58
1-16

"The novice should be clearly told all the hardships and difficulties that will lead him to God."

58:8

☙

Most of us in the West live in a society that seeks instant gratification. We live in a world of instant rice, instant oatmeal, instant coffee, and an instant version of just about anything you can think of. We even have drive-through churches, and if you don't want to have to travel, you can download your "Instant Karma" on your smart phone.

Saint Benedict reminds us that some things are not meant to be instant, especially things of the soul. It takes time to build a strong foundation for the spiritual life. There are no short cuts; we must "pay our dues" if we desire spiritual growth. If we are willing to be patient and invest sufficient time, the Lord promises to form us into the persons we are meant to be. Saint Benedict learned this principle from his own experience as a hermit, from his serving as an abbot in communal monastic life, and from his reading the works of the "desert fathers." This formation involves a process of slowing down and not taking life for granted. When life is lived in this way, its blessings become easier to recognize, and we begin to live in a spirit of praise, thanksgiving, and joy, a spirit which overflows into loving service of others.

Mark Dittmer

CHAPTER 58
17-29

"When he is to be received, [the novice] comes before the whole community in the oratory and promises stability, fidelity to monastic life, and obedience."

58:17

☙

THE LATIN PHRASE that corresponds to "fidelity to monastic life" is *conversatio morum suorum*, a complex phrase that can also be translated as "conversion of life in the monastic manner," that is, a life subject to the *Rule* of Saint Benedict and the way it is lived by monks in a particular community. This way of life involves praying the Divine Office with the other monks; but even more, it means using the *Rule* and the inspiration of Saint Benedict to turn away from sin and towards God in constant conversion. It includes overcoming bad habits of thought, emotion, and speech; confronting the darkness within ourselves; and surrendering to the need to change as prompted by the Holy Spirit. *Conversatio* also commits us to daily communion with God in prayer and to the pursuit of growth in holiness through practice of the steps of humility.

A Benedictine community is an ongoing source of mutual support and encouragement as its members respond to Christ's call to "come, follow Me" (Mt 4:19) through the surprises and changes of daily life. Those who follow the *Rule* seek to run in the sweetness of God's commands by going about doing good works of service and thereby growing in communion with God and with our fellow Oblates and monks. We are reassured in knowing that we are united with other Oblates and monks in the common struggle to imitate Jesus, who humbled Himself and became obedient to death, even to death on a cross (cf. Phil 2:8).

Fr. Aaron Buzzelli, O.S.B.

CHAPTER 59
1-8

"[A parent] offers his son to God in the monastery ..."

59:1

☙

THE OFFERING OF one's self is the greatest offering to be made to the Lord. We are giving back to God what is already His. We are His. We are His people. The offering of ourselves back to God in gratitude is the ultimate acknowledgment to the Lord of His taking us on as His own. He welcomes joyfully those who are surfeited with material goods as well as those who are in city slums or in the backwoods of any forest or jungle. He makes no distinction regarding externals, since it is what is in the offered soul that matters to Our Lord.

The offering of one's child, the fruit of a mother's womb, to the Lord in the sacrament of Baptism is the offering of the closest, most intimate part of ourselves to Him. When we make this offering, we are imitating God in His giving of His Son – His only Son – to us. We are asking God to guide our children as He guided His Son; to show our children the way back to His arms as He directed His Son; and to answer our children's prayers as He answered His Son's. We cannot do it ourselves; only with many graces can our children mature as true children of our heavenly Father in the way of Christ. Let us, then, offer our children to God wholeheartedly, both in Baptism and in all our dealings with them during their formative years.

LORA ANNE JACOB

CHAPTER 60
1-9

"If an ordained priest asks to be received into the monastery, do not agree too quickly."

60:1

❦

On the surface Saint Benedict seems very reluctant to admit priests into monastic life. He directs the abbot not to be too quick to receive a priest, and he stresses the importance of discerning the motives of a priest who seeks to enter the monastery. If a priest is received, it is made very clear that no favoritism is to be shown to him; he begins at the lowest rank just as any other member begins.

Saint Benedict is not being anti-clerical or unreasonably strict with these instructions. Rather, he had no doubt learned from experience that the call to religious life and the call to priesthood are two different calls and that each has its particular characteristics. A priest who seeks to enter a monastery has been formed to be a diocesan priest, and this formation molds him to be independent in his daily life and personally responsible for his material needs. On the other hand, the call to religious life involves a different formation. It is a formation directed toward living in community, which involves surrendering one's daily freedom to the wisdom of the abbot and following the daily schedule of the monastery. It involves praying together, working together, eating together, recreating together, and living in common.

I am mindful of this difference as I make the transition from being a diocesan priest to living as a monk; I can see how the formation is very different. In some ways I can relate to Blessed Teresa of Calcutta, who described her move from belonging to the Sisters of Loreto to founding the Missionaries of Charity as her "call within a call."

This "call within a call" involves formation. It is important to recognize the need for formation; otherwise there is the danger of having a diocesan priest dressed as a Benedictine but still living the life of a diocesan priest. This lack of integrity would not be good for either the monastery or the priest. Benedictine formation is meant to form or re-form our lives around the *Rule* of Saint Benedict. Whether we do this as a monk on the way to formal profession in a monastic community, as an Oblate of Saint Benedict, or as someone else who simply wants to grow spiritually through incorporating Benedictine values, it must be done with an openness to change. This formation involves entering freely into the call and allowing ourselves to be brought closer to the Lord by embracing the *Holy Rule* and its values and disciplines.

Fr. Killian Loch, O.S.B.

CHAPTER 61
1-5

"A visiting monk from far away ... [ought to be] content with the life as he finds it ..."

61:1, 2

☙

WHAT DOES AN ancient rule concerning the reception of visiting monks have to say to an Oblate in the twenty-first century? On reflection, it speaks to me as a father, father-in-law, step-father, brother, and brother-in-law who is sometimes a guest in another's home and sometimes a host in my own.

As a guest, am I content with the life in the home as I find it? Do I make excessive demands? If I perceive some defect or fault, what do I say? Furthermore, how do I receive criticism from <u>my</u> guests? The *Rule* provides a guide when it says that criticism or observations should be made with humility and love. It indicates that the host has the final authority to judge the validity of such criticism or observation.

Within this past fortnight, I have been both a guest and a host. Both experiences were filled with joy and provided me with delightful memories. Reflection on the wisdom of this chapter of the *Rule* would probably have improved both experiences.

This passage also has a broader application beyond extending and receiving hospitality. For my part, this includes the need promptly to put on the virtues of humility and love as soon as thoughts of criticism enter my mind. There is a part of my personality that wants to put on white gloves, so to speak, and inspect for dust in hidden nooks – that is, other people's nooks. I pray for the grace to put away those inspector's gloves and to put on the apron of a humble laborer who depends upon the generosity of the Master for my daily wage.

JAMES PENNELL

CHAPTER 61
6-14

"... so that others may learn from his example ..."

61:9

☙

IT SEEMS AMAZING that, considering the great importance of the vow of stability, Saint Benedict should recommend that a visiting monk be received as a member of a host community if he is judged to be of good character. We may assume that the context of this provision may have been a "vocation visit"; that is, the visiting monk was prayerfully questioning his place in his current community and was visiting specifically to discern whether God might be calling him to join the host monastery. Perhaps, as is sometimes the case today, his home monastery was in the process of being dissolved or was plagued by poor observance. In any case, Saint Benedict states that an observant monk from another community "should even be urged to stay, so that others may learn from his example" (61:9), provided that he has permission from the abbot of the monk's original community (cf. 61:13).

The phrase about the monk's good example may remind us of the many people in our lives who have provided us with edifying words and behavior, especially in the practice of our faith. Have not parents, grandparents, aunts, uncles, and sometimes siblings nurtured our faith in powerful ways, whether we realized it at the time or not? Have not close friends steered us away from bad decisions and evil paths? Have not fellow monks and fellow Oblates inspired us by their caring, faith-filled words or by their generous, self-giving actions? Have not fellow employees helped to renew us in our faithful acceptance of difficult tasks by their own uncomplaining perseverance in undesirable work? In our prayer let us offer thanks for such people. Let us often remember the good examples from our past lives, and let us be aware, with thanks and praise, that God has sent these people into our lives to help us in our vocations and to lead us reliably to sanctification. Let us likewise seek to provide good Christian example to others in all that we say or do.

Fr. Donald Raila, O.S.B.

CHAPTER 62
1-11

"[The priest] must be on guard against conceit or pride" and must "make more and more progress toward God"

62:2, 4

☙

SAINT BENEDICT CLEARLY has respect for the office of priesthood, but he also shows great caution concerning the possibility of priests' becoming proud and demanding and thus disrupting the peace of the monastic community. In his monastery, most monks, including Saint Benedict himself, were not priests; so those who <u>were</u> ordained might easily have been tempted to think of themselves as privileged and to expect exceptional treatment. In both Chapters 60 and 62 of the *Rule*, Saint Benedict felt compelled to state that priests should be received only reluctantly, that they must be subject to the discipline of the *Rule* and to obedience to the abbot, and that they should not make exceptions for themselves. Furthermore, a priest who has consistently not observed the *Rule* "must be regarded as a rebel, not as a priest" (62:8). That is strong language! There are similar warnings about deans' becoming "puffed up with ... pride" (19:5), about cellarers' treating people with disdain (31:7), and about priors' being "led astray by conceit and [growing] proud" (65:18). All these passages indicate that people in authority can easily be misled into abusing their God-given positions.

All of us who have positions of authority should take heed. Our Lord often chastens the scribes and Pharisees for their lack of living faith and for abuses of their spiritual authority.

Anyone with temporal or spiritual authority over others is likely to experience temptations to pride, to abuse of power, and to excessive self-esteem. If we have been mistreated by someone in authority, we are called to forgive and, if necessary, to seek healing. Also, whatever authority we have, it is to be exercised with kindness and humility. We need to avoid the bad examples given to us in the past. We need to "be on guard against conceit or pride" (62:2). We need to recognize our position as a genuine gift from God, bestowed on us so that we may serve in the name of Christ and with His own self-sacrificing love. Christ is our one perfect example of authority; He ruled by serving and died for His flock in order to save them from sin and death and to bring them into eternal life with the Blessed Trinity.

FR. DONALD RAILA, O.S.B.

CHAPTER 63
1-9

"Let all keep their places in the monastery established by the time of their entrance, the merit of their lives and the decision of the Abbot"

63:1; Leonard J. Doyle trans.

☙❧

WHAT DETERMINES OUR status, particularly in a society so inundated with the influence of social media? Wherein does our human dignity lie? Rank in the community is not something that is arbitrary or derived from a bygone era and an antiquated society; rather it is integral to the process of teaching us humility and the proper dignity to be shown to one another. Note the three factors involved: the date of entry, virtue of life, and the decision of the abbot.

Rank is primarily a factor of timing. Some of us are the oldest, and some the youngest; we do not choose. God chooses for His own purposes. Are we willing to accept the place He has designated for us? Do we lord over others because of our position?

Rank should not keep us from living out a holy life. We are called to live a virtuous life where we are and in the position in which we find ourselves. How can I live a virtuous life and be a good example for those around me, regardless of my status? Do I let my status depress me, or do I find opportunities for good within the given limitations?

Rank should be changed only by another. We do not determine our rank, but are rewarded for a life lived well. Is our living authentic, or are we seeking simply to advance ourselves through lies and deception? How would changing my rank affect those around me? Would they be jealous, or would there be real concern? Am I humble or proud? Is this God's will or my own?

Br. Isaac Haywiser, O.S.B.

CHAPTER 63
10-19

"The juniors, therefore, should honor their
seniors, and the seniors love their juniors."
63:10; Leonard J. Doyle trans.

☙

IN A SOCIETY of declining moral values and greater disregard for the elderly, we are challenged to hold on to the respect and decorum that acknowledge a ranking of honor. Do we, if we are youthful, follow society's indifferent tendencies and disregard the elderly because we think we know better; or do we listen to them and learn from them? Do we, if we are elderly, hold back wisdom and advice because we judge that the youth are not willing to listen and are impossibly different from the youth of days gone by? Do we respect the youth and treat them as responsible members of society? Do we all set an example for others? Do we judge another because he is not from our era of time and may differ from us in understanding or experience? Do we show respect for the dignity of the other in external expression?

The challenge here is to see Christ in the other and to respect the great responsibility and experience of the elderly as well as the ingenuity and energetic zeal that the young bring to the family and community. Mutual respect is crucial and necessary for living out life in Christian community or family. We must overcome the tendency of society to question absolutely everything, particularly those things which have survived the test of time. We must learn once again to listen to one another, to both the old and the young, and seek to make time for mutual discourse so that we can all grow and learn – for our benefit and for the glory of God.

Br. Isaac Haywiser, O.S.B.

CHAPTER 64
1-6

"Goodness of life and wisdom in teaching must be the criteria for choosing the one to be made abbot ..."

64:2

☙

WE SEE IN these verses Saint Benedict's great concern for the proper ordering of the community. The abbot is to be chosen for goodness of life and wisdom of teaching – high qualities distilled from Benedict's experience.

In Saint Pachomius' rule and in the *Rule of the Master*, the abbot leaving office designated his successor. Benedict, in contrast, saw the abbot as a charismatic spiritual father and regarded the community as the best judge of God's will in the choice of an abbot (cf. *RB 1980*, Appendix 2). The election that Benedict prescribes may reflect his conception of a monastery where the monks, "armed with the strong and noble weapons of obedience to do battle for the true King, Christ the Lord" (Prol: 3), become capable of choosing the one who will rule them.

Probably it was Saint Benedict's inspired love of the ordered beauty that Christ's presence brings to a community that led him to prescribe such extreme remedies (in *RB* 64:3-6) for the removal of an evil abbot – by other abbots, by the bishop, or even by the faithful local people. The election might then be determined by "some [small] part of the community" (64:1), if they posses sounder judgment. Remedies today may differ, but Benedict's perennial wisdom was the clear vision that stern, unpalatable remedies, applied appropriately, would allow the community to move forward – perhaps chastened and with some sorrow, but in a reestablished peace and with a greater capacity to "prefer nothing to the love of Christ" (cf. 4:21).

CLARE GODT

CHAPTER 64
7-22

"[The abbot] must show forethought and consideration in his orders, and… should be discerning and moderate …"

64:17

☙

ONCE IN OFFICE, the abbot must keep in mind the burden he has received and remember to Whom he is accountable – God Himself. The same applies to a teacher, who in her role as educator is also ultimately accountable to God, our true Superior. Our goal as teachers must be to bring out what is best in our pupils. We must be temperate and merciful and love our students despite their faults.

When correction is necessary, we must be wise and listen with the ear of our hearts. We who are teachers must not strive so hard to change our pupils' ways that we crush their spirits or individual initiative. An abbot, like a good biological father or a teacher, should wish to be loved rather than feared. Forethought and consideration of others' needs should be shown; thus we who are teachers need to be faithful to attending council meetings and making lesson plans. Abbots and teachers must be discerning and moderate, with the realization that our brother monks or students have come from God and belong to God. As Saint Benedict asserts in quoting holy Jacob, "*If I drive my flocks too hard, they will all die in a single day*" (64:18; Gen 33:13). Teachers and abbots alike must allow the stronger something to yearn for and prevent the weaker from running away. Such a balance is learned by a wise abbot and by a good teacher.

Abbots and teachers, who are so very similar in their vocations, should serve their communities unselfishly, strive to cooperate with others, minister with their hearts as well as with their minds and hands, and ultimately make spiritual progress themselves as they seek the growth of others.

DANA GRASHA

CHAPTER 64
7-22

"He [the abbot] should always *let mercy triumph over judgment* (Jas 2:13) so that he too may win mercy. He must hate faults but love the brothers."

64:10-11

☙

BENEDICT DOES NOT imagine the abbot to be like an Old Testament patriarch; rather he sees the abbot of the monastery as someone like the father in the parable of the prodigal son in Saint Luke's Gospel. The father loves both his sons equally, the one who appears to remain strong in his fidelity as much as the one who squanders his life and returns seeking forgiveness. The father recognizes the unique qualities and personality of each son and tries to bring each into a harmonious, familial climate.

Thus the abbot is a loving, compassionate father, capable of both encouragement and discipline and zealous for the eternal well-being of those in his care. Even amid the strict conditions that make monastic life an unsustainable burden for some monks, the abbot is both a source of divine grace and an image of God's presence who supports and sustains the community and its individual members. He compassionately leads all to the full reward promised to faithful disciples.

BR. DAVID KELLY, O.S.B.

CHAPTER 65
1-10

"Some priors, puffed up by the evil spirit of pride and thinking of themselves as second abbots, usurp tyrannical power and foster contention and discord in their communities."

65:2

☙

ONE OF MY favorite childhood stories is that of "Yertle the Turtle" by Dr. Seuss. Yertle, king of the turtles, desired to rule beyond the pond where he lived. Believing he was king of all that he could see, he was raised to greater heights on the backs of the other turtles. He was brought low when Mack, a small turtle on the bottom of the pile, caved in under the strain. Yertle became "King of the Mud," and the turtles returned to their peaceful life.

The prior in this passage also loses perspective. Regardless of who appoints the prior, he will need to give an account of his stewardship to God, just as the abbot does (*RB* 64:7). Leadership, regardless of whether it is assigned or given informally, is a trust from God. Saint Benedict's instruction to the prior applies to us if we are to keep a proper perspective regarding our duties. We can carry out our assignments respectfully, put the interests of others before our own, be willing to do the will of another, and be mindful of the *Rule*, whose wisdom guides us in our life with God. The values of the *Rule* will not deliver us from the difficulties that accompany leadership, but will keep us mindful of God and help us lead people along the path of life and light.

SUSAN WYKOFF

CHAPTER 65
11-22

> "Yet the abbot should reflect that he must give God an account of all his judgments …"
>
> *65:22*

❧

SAINT BENEDICT CLEARLY establishes the abbot as the unchallenged superior of a monastery, but he also realizes that abbots have to share their authority and responsibilities with others, foremost among whom is the prior. To make sure that this balancing act succeeds, Benedict strongly cautions the prior not to be inflated with pride over his sharing in the abbot's clout, nor to set his eyes on his boss's job. At the same time, at the end of the sixty-fifth chapter of the *Rule*, Benedict counsels the abbot not to be harsh with the prior, for the abbot will eventually have to "give an account" of his judgments and actions to God.

The phrase "to give an account" occurs numerous times in the *Rule*, almost always with reference to the abbot. It seems to be a reminder that Benedict employed to further the goal of encouraging mutual respect between the abbot and his brothers in Christ. Working co-operatively with others can be difficult; Benedict's advice to remember that we will all one day "give an account" of our stewardship can help us to work together in harmony for the good of all who frequent the school of the Lord's service.

FR. EDWARD MAZICH, O.S.B.

Chapter 66
1-8

> "As soon as anyone knocks, or a poor man calls out, he [the porter] replies, 'Thanks be to God' or 'Your blessing, please' … "
>
> 66:3

☙

Just as a monastery houses the collective souls of its monks and guests, so do our hearts serve as abodes to whatever we allow to enter. To whom or what shall we allow entry? Who will be our doorkeeper?

The *Holy Rule* tells us that the porter should be one who is reliable and discerning, one who would lovingly allow entry to the virtuous and, by implication, refuse admittance in a kind manner to any kind of evil. Who should be assigned to this post?

From our birth, the constant guardian of our soul has been our guardian angel, who serves the divine will of the Father. We also rely on the aid of our Blessed Mother and other special saints who work with our angel to lead us on the way of salvation. When we accept such guidance, our hearts will be able to receive whomever or whatever we need to obtain the mercy and graces of God, coming to us bountifully through Jesus Christ. We need to search no further.

Teresa D. Warlow

CHAPTER 67
1-7

"All absent brothers should always be remembered at the closing prayer of the Work of God."

67:2

☙

THIS CHAPTER INDICATES that travel presents hazards and that they must be addressed. Benedictine commentators point out the physical hazards encountered in travel in sixth-century Italy, but even more emphasize the moral hazards likely to spring up on the way. Most especially, prayer is important both for the travelers and for the community remaining at home. Prayers should be offered both before travel, for protection and guidance, and after travel, for thanksgiving for safety and deliverance from any evil encountered.

A traveler is temporarily removed from the familiar supportive surroundings of his or her Christian way of life. Unfamiliar, unsupportive, and perhaps even evil elements of a different environment are encountered, and these tend to challenge the traveler very directly. Harmful elements are best avoided, but when avoidance is not possible, especially in regard to people, charity toward them is essential. As Dom Hubert van Zeller points out, charity is one major purpose of monastic travel.

Christian living is a circumscribed way of life in that it avoids evil and seeks always to nurture the interior spiritual life. To this end, prayer and silence should be practiced during travel; these practices can be readily maintained especially when one is traveling alone.

BR. HUGH LESTER, O.S.B.

CHAPTER 68
1-5

"If ... the superior is still determined to hold to his original order, then the junior must recognize that this is best for him. Trusting in God's help, he must in love obey."

68:4-5

☙

TO ACCEPT A work assignment with perfect obedience to a human superior is to manifest trust in God. The nature of the work itself is not really important; it might be a task that is irritating or boring, a problem that is difficult to solve, or a burden that is heavy to bear. Whether the task is agreeable or not, it offers an opportunity to show perfect obedience, which is grounded in love. To be moved by love means that we can accept seemingly impossible things since they become possible with the help of our omnipotent God. It is the nature of a humble and simple heart to accept in obedience whatever is assigned. A humble heart, freed from pride, is able to recognize that despite human nature's limitations of strength and will, the power that comes with faith in God enables us to surpass our own nature and to accomplish almost any sort of task.

Saint Benedict wants obedience and gentleness from his brothers not because he wishes them to accept heavy burdens but because he is concerned with the sanctification and salvation of each brother. When committed by love to do whatever work is given, people can grow in virtue and experience daily conversion. The exemplary human life of Jesus, constituting the Father's plan of human salvation, exhibited perfect obedience to His Father. His sacrifice on the cross would appear to be an impossibly cruel mission for any human being, but because of His loving obedience to the Father, His love for us, and His desire for our salvation, Jesus freely accepted the cross and thus brought about the redemption of all mankind.

Br. Martinho Zevallos, O.S.B.

CHAPTER 69
1-4

> "[Defending another monk] can be a most serious source and occasion of contention."
>
> 69:3

☙

AT FIRST GLANCE, this chapter may seem to be among the least relevant to us. Who, we might think, would be defending another monk against any charges? Furthermore, what is wrong with defending someone if justice is on our side?

The context of this passage is undoubtedly the imposition of a prescribed penalty on a misbehaving monk. That monk, therefore, is undergoing "therapy" approved by the abbot to correct some disruptive behavior. If so, another monk does no good by presuming to champion the cause of someone who has already been "judged and sentenced" in an acceptable manner. In fact, to try to overturn an approved decision can only cause contention in the community and detract from its unity and peace. Corrections and penalties are not always a bad thing!

Any of us might feel moved to intervene when one of our family members or friends is accused of wrongdoing. We need to be very careful not to let our emotions or blood ties control our response to the situation. Very often it is best to let our loved one suffer the consequences of his or her improper behavior. There are times in families and communities when we best show love for others by not interfering in business that is not explicitly ours. We need to love, pray, and provide good Christian example. It is thus that we most effectively cooperate with God's graces to bring about healing and conversion in someone who is dear to us.

Fr. Donald Raila, O.S.B.

CHAPTER 70
1-7

"[Control and supervision must be] done
with moderation and common sense."

70:5

☙

AS HE DOES in Chapter 69, Saint Benedict here warns against "presumption," this time regarding the imposition of punishments. Once again, self-restraint in this matter is the proper response if one has no authority to administer penalties. One must trust in the process established by the community to have only the abbot, or those appointed by him, administer discipline.

If one <u>has</u> authority to mete out discipline, as in the case of monks' dealing with younger boys, even then the supervision of behavior must be exercised "with moderation and common sense" (70:5). All too often people with issues of their own readily become enraged at others' supposed misbehavior. Some people (and perhaps there is some of this tendency in all of us) tend to be critical, quick to condemn, and ready to see themselves as judges and juries. Those who have such excessive inclinations must themselves be restrained and disciplined, if not by themselves then by others.

This legislation of Saint Benedict is meant to preserve good order and charity in a community. Penalties are sometimes required, but they need to be imposed reluctantly and reasonably. They are imposed not out of spite or vengeance but for the sake of helping the offender to make progress in his journey of ongoing conversion. The penalties should also help to preserve the community's capacity to live in the peace of Christ. May we all, then, hold in check our inclinations to judge, criticize, and clamor for punishment. Let us subject such impulses to prayer and reason, even if we do have authority over others. Let us strive to see others with eyes of love and nurture a desire to bring others closer to Christ. As Our Lord commands in the Gospel, "Judge not lest you be judged" (cf. Mt 7:1).

Fr. Donald Raila, O.S.B.

CHAPTER 71
1-9

"Obedience is a blessing to be shown by all, not only to the abbot but also to one another as brothers, since we know that it is by this way of obedience that we go to God."

71:1-2

☙

MUTUAL OBEDIENCE IS probably not something which is a high priority in most people's lives. We may feel obliged to show obedience to our employers or superiors out of duty or perhaps out of fear of punishment. Saint Benedict, however, calls for a mutual obedience which emphasizes the relational nature which exists among persons. All of us, as members of the Body of Christ, need always to be listening to one another and to be attentive to one another's needs. At the same time, Saint Benedict goes on to acknowledge that in the monastery there is a hierarchy and that the orders of those who are appointed over us must take precedence since the superiors have the very particular responsibility of acting in the person of Christ, who deserves our love and respect.

The world in which we live would certainly be a much gentler place if we learned the lesson that respect is not earned but rather due to each and every person because we are all God's children. Furthermore, this respect is commanded by Christ. May we listen carefully to the needs of all around us, from the youngest to the eldest, and may we take these needs to heart.

FR. JEFFREY S. NYARDY, O. S. B.

CHAPTER 72
1-12

"This, then, is the good zeal which monks must foster with fervent love …"

72:3

☙❧

IN CHAPTER 72 of the *Rule*, Saint Benedict addresses the crucial question of a wicked zeal, which separates from God, and a good zeal, which leads to God. The good zeal, Benedict says, the monks must foster with fervent love in order to overcome the attraction of a wicked zeal in a community. Throughout the *Rule* Benedict shows that he is well aware of the Biblical revelation of original sin. Because of choices to be separated from God, their Creator, humans have fallen into a state of slavery to the fear of death, from which they do not have the power to free themselves. Preservation of one's own life becomes the ultimate value in hostile competition with other people in keeping death at bay. Whatever serves that ultimate purpose is judged to be good; killing, stealing, deceit, and the like become acceptable means of obtaining the power and possession necessary to make one's own life more secure. This is the work of wicked zeal.

Into the fallen condition of humanity, Jesus, the Son of God, comes with the good news of the divine gift of liberation. The Letter to the Hebrews (2:14-15) gives a summary of this good news, which is told in various ways throughout the New Testament: "Now since the children share in blood and flesh, he [Jesus] likewise shared in them, that through death he might destroy the one who has the power of death, that is, the devil, and free those who through fear of death had been subject to slavery all their life."

The *Rule* of Saint Benedict is a celebration of the good news of Jesus Christ, who came to live with us. Now in communion of life in the freedom and good zeal of the Risen Lord, we are able to do the work of good zeal, which is love. The last sentence of Chapter 72 forms a kind of prayer and summarizes Benedict's essential purpose in writing his *Rule*: "Let them prefer nothing whatever to Christ, and may he bring us all together to everlasting life" (72:11-12).

ARCHABBOT DOUGLAS R. NOWICKI, O.S.B.

CHAPTER 72
1-12

"Let them prefer nothing whatever to Christ …"

72:11

☙

SOME COMMENTATORS SAY that Chapter 72 might be considered a synthesis of the entire *Rule*. As one of them has stated, Saint Benedict, in a few short sentences, summarizes the whole doctrine of monastic perfection. As for me, I feel as if I am meeting the man Saint Benedict in this chapter. Every word of it penetrates to the most interior attitude and to the deepest motives of the heart as we are challenged to live a good life in community according to our particular vocation.

There is so much here that I could spend a year reflecting on this one chapter alone. I look at it as a holy lamp in my possession; like the ten virgins in Saint Matthew's Gospel, I have a choice either to see an opportunity, by the power of the Holy Spirit, to fill my lamp with oil as did the five wise virgins, or to be caught empty at the Lord's coming at midnight, because I have not taken to heart what it means to prefer nothing to Christ. When the Lord comes, I do not want to hear the words, "I do not know you." What, then, is the oil for my lamp?

Saint Benedict identifies the evil zeal of bitterness only as that which leads to damnation. I think it is a fair assumption to say that the fruit of evil zeal would be corruption. Bitterness can do that. The Letter to the Hebrews cautions us "that no 'root of bitterness' spring up and cause trouble" (Heb 11:15). Evil zeal has a way of spreading like an uncontrollable virus. It doesn't respond to the best antibiotics because the person promoting it has mounted a defense to justify the reasons for his frenetic fervor, like a world-class prosecutor. One can't win against his tactics. Therefore, nix that for the lamp!

Conversely, good zeal "separates from vice and leads to God." And what is that? Good zeal is charity in full activity. In reality, it is that which inspires mutual kindness, which in turn supports a neighbor's faults of character and bodily infirmities with an attitude of peaceable, affectionate patience. It renders obedience easy. It triumphs over egotism, which is the self-seeking that makes us prefer what is useful to oneself over that which is useful to another. The *Commentary for Benedictine Oblates* by G.A. Simon states, "Without good zeal the virtues are somewhat constrained, forced; sometimes they are not even anything but the appearance of virtues" (page 503).

Now you see why I could spend a year on this. In my vocation as a married woman, mother, grandmother, daughter, niece, cousin, etc., I don't even have to let my feet touch the floor in the morning before I've already asked for forgiveness and the grace to find charity through obedience. At each moment I need to let the Holy Spirit come in and provide the needed oil for my lamp. The only way to arrive at the desired results is to recognize that solely through His power can I learn to put Christ above all and give myself completely over, in love, to God and to my neighbor because I hold nothing back. I must prefer absolutely nothing to Christ. Only a supernatural work can produce more than the appearance of virtues. I guarantee you: the oil for my lamp is not coming from my fleshly efforts. Left to myself, I will surely think "the bridegroom is long delayed" and then become drowsy and fall asleep. Today is the day to sing to the Lord and ask:

"Give me oil in my lamp, keep me burning.
Give me oil in my lamp, I pray.
Give me oil in my lamp, keep me burning.
Keep me burning 'til the break of day."

   —from *Child Bible Songs,*
      given on the website childbiblesongs.com.

CAROLYN VAN PELT

CHAPTER 73
1-9

"The reason we have written this rule is that, by observing it in monasteries, we can show that we have some degree of virtue and the beginnings of monastic life."

73:1

༼༽

IN THIS FINAL chapter of the *Rule*, Saint Benedict tells us that his rule is the "least of rules, which we have drawn up for beginners." He comments that there are other paths that those who have reached a higher degree of perfection in the spiritual life may follow. Those who sincerely seek God always have a desire for a more perfect relationship with Him. Perfection is the ideal for which they strive. We would like to soar with the angels.

However, one of the things that we experience as monastics and Oblates is the feeling that we are always starting over in our spiritual life, that we are beginning again and again and taking only "baby steps." In the monastery there used to be what was called a "chapter of faults," during which each monk examined his life to see just where he stood on the road to perfection and then reported his faults to the community. Although one may not have liked this custom, nevertheless it could have served the purpose of making each monk realize that, if he had begun to think very highly of himself, in reality he had not come very far in the quest for perfection. It was a way of humbling oneself. Saint Benedict understood the desire that some people have to exalt themselves regarding their spiritual growth. He addresses this temptation with the simple directive: "Do not desire to be called holy before you actually are" (cf. 4:62).

Finally, we must remember that our spiritual growth is dependent on God's working through us. It is only by cooperating with God in His work that we can arrive at the state of being "full of grace" as was the Blessed Virgin Mary. Our Blessed Mother readily gave credit to God for whatever she had become when she said in her Magnificat, "The Almighty has done great things for me" (Lk 1:49). May we pray, "Lord God, give us humility to do the same. Amen."

Fr. Ronald Gatman, O.S.B.

Appendices

THE FOLLOWING "**Rule** of Love" was submitted by Oblate Dana Grasha. She comments, "Every good work should begin with prayer. My 'Rule of Love' was read each morning before classes began. The students, 7th and 8th-graders, took turns reading it. I used this for many years. ... I call it the 'Rule of Love' because without a ground work of love, nothing can be taught or learned." She compiled this as a paraphrase of the Prologue of the *Rule*.

RULE OF LOVE

Listen, my children, and with all your heart hear the principles of your God. Readily accept and faithfully follow the advice of a loving Father, so that through obedience you may return to Him from whom you came. My words are meant for you, whoever you are.

Serve Him always with your God-given talents so that you may inherit His Kingdom and follow Him to glory. "Come, you children, and listen to Me: I will teach you the fear of the Lord." Run where you have the light; live what God wills in your lifetime, while you have the ability and the chance.

We are about to open a school for God's service, in which we hope nothing harsh or oppressive will be directed; for preserving charity or correcting faults, it may be necessary at times, by reason of justice, to be slightly more severe. Do not fear this and retreat, for the path of salvation is long and the entrance narrow.

As our lives and faith progress, the heart expands, and with sweetness of love we move down the paths of God's commandments. Never departing from His guidance, we patiently share in Christ's passion, so that we may eventually enter into the Kingdom of God!

Contributor Biographies

A

Fr. Thomas Acklin, O.S.B., has been a professed monk of St. Vincent Archabbey since 1975. He currently serves as chaplain at St. Emma Monastery and professor of systematic theology at St. Vincent Seminary.

Br. Pio Adamonis, O.S.B., has been a professed monk of St. Vincent Archabbey since 2009. He is currently a student at St. Vincent Seminary. He also serves as an assistant sacristan/master of ceremonies for the monastery, works for the Archabbey/Seminary Public Relations Department, and serves as the assistant coach for men's and women's golf teams of St. Vincent College.

Fr. Shawn Matthew Anderson, O.S.B., has been a professed monk of Saint Vincent Archabbey since 2002. He teaches in the Biology Department at St. Vincent College.

Fr. Michael Antonacci, O.S.B., has been a professed monk of St. Vincent Archabbey since 2008. A full-time student at St. Vincent Seminary, he was ordained to the diaconate in April, 2013, and was ordained a priest in May, 2014. He also works as an assistant in the Physics Department at St. Vincent College.

B

Fr. William A. Beaver, O.S.B., has been a professed monk of St. Vincent Archabbey since 1981.

FR. KURT BELSOLE, O.S.B., has been a professed monk of St. Vincent Archabbey since 1972. He currently serves as the Director of Liturgy of the North American College (seminary) in Rome.

CHRISTOPHER BROWN of Alamo, GA, has been an Oblate of St. Benedict affiliated with St. Vincent Archabbey since July 11, 2013.

FR. AARON BUZZELLI, O.S.B., has been a professed monk of St. Vincent Archabbey since 1972. He currently serves as the Director of Spiritual Life at St. Vincent Seminary, as the assistant Director of the Mission Office of the Archabbey, and as an archivist for the monastery.

C

FR. ANDREW CAMPBELL, O.S.B., has been a professed monk of St. Vincent Archabbey since 1977. He currently works in the office of Archabbey/Seminary Public Relations, is in charge of the Archabbey's website, and serves as archivist for the Archabbey.

DARRAN CHICK of Waynesburg, PA, has been an Oblate of St. Benedict affiliated with St. Vincent Archabbey since September 29, 2013.

DONNA CIARCINSKI of Monroeville, PA, has been an Oblate of St. Benedict affiliated with St. Vincent Archabbey since 1991.

JOSEPH C. CIRELLI of Coraopolis, PA, has been an Oblate of St. Benedict affiliated with St. Vincent Archabbey since November, 1989. He is also a Marine Corps veteran, a retired President/CEO of the Clearview Federal Credit Union, and a member of St. Malachy Parish, Kennedy Township, PA.

FR. VINCENT DE PAUL CROSBY, O.S.B., has been a professed monk of St. Vincent Archabbey since 1968. He is also an artist and currently serves as the Director of Archabbey Studios.

D

DIANA MARTIN of Dilliner, PA, has been an Oblate of St. Benedict affiliated with St. Vincent Archabbey since 2010.

MARK DITTMER of St. Gabriel, LA, has been an Oblate affiliated with St. Vincent Archabbey since 2011.

JOSEPH DUCHENE of Washington, DC, was a monk of St. Vincent Archabbey from 2009 to 2013 and was known as Br. Romuald, O.S.B.

E

SUZANNE ENGLISH of Latrobe, PA, works at Saint Vincent College. She is a professed Secular Franciscan who regularly attends Oblate meetings in Latrobe to deepen her understanding of Benedictine spirituality.

F

Debra Ann Femia of Coal Center, PA, has been an Oblate of St. Benedict affiliated with St. Vincent Archabbey since 2002.

Fr. Chad Ficorilli, O.S.B., has been a professed monk of St. Vincent Archabbey since July, 1974. He currently serves as Catholic chaplain at Excela Westmoreland Hospital in Greensburg, PA.

Dr. Richard Fitzgerald of Mt. Pleasant, SC, has been an Oblate of St. Benedict affiliated with St. Vincent Archabbey since 2007. He is a medical doctor who often assists the monks at Mepkin Abbey in South Carolina.

Paul Fling of Myrtle Beach, SC, has been an Oblate of St. Benedict affiliated with St. Vincent Archabbey since 2011.

Jeffrey Fountaine of Exeter, PA, has been an Oblate of St. Benedict affiliated with St. Vincent Archabbey since 2008.

G

Fr. Ronald Gatman, O.S.B., has been a professed monk of St. Vincent Archabbey since 1974. He currently serves as the full-time Director of Campus Ministry of Benedictine Military School in Savannah, Georgia, and as moderator of the Savannah Deanery of Oblates.

Clare Godt of Pittsburgh, PA, has been an Oblate of St. Benedict affiliated with St. Vincent Archabbey since 2012.

CONTRIBUTOR BIOGRAPHIES

DANA GRASHA of Parma, OH, has been an Oblate of St. Benedict affiliated with St. Vincent Archabbey since 1989. She is currently retired from teaching grades 7-12 and "has been a friend to St. Vincent Archabbey and St. Vincent College since she was four years old, back in the days of Fr. Mark Kistner, Bishop Rene Gracida, and Fr. Anthony Burlas." She says further that she has been blessed with so many memories that she "could write a book."

H

FR. THOMAS HART, O.S.B., has been a professed monk of St. Vincent Archabbey since 1984. He currently serves as an instructor in the Theology Department at St. Vincent College and as Assistant to the President (of the college) for Mission.

BR. ISAAC HAYWISER, O.S.B., has been a professed monk of St. Vincent Archabbey since 2010. He currently is a full-time student at St. Vincent Seminary, works at the St. Vincent Book Center, and serves as an assistant sacristan/master of ceremonies for the monastery.

BR. BRUNO HEISEY, O.S.B., has been a professed monk of St. Vincent Archabbey since 2002. He teaches Church history at St. Vincent Seminary and is the author of several books and numerous articles in journals.

FR. BONIFACE HICKS, O.S.B., has been a professed monk of Saint Vincent Archabbey since 1999. He currently serves as the program manager of Catholic Radio Station WAOB ("We Are One Body") and regularly gives numerous retreats and days of recollection.

Rev. Joel Hummel of Hanover, PA, has been an Oblate of St. Benedict affiliated with St. Vincent Archabbey since 2012. He is a minister in the United Church of Christ and serves as chaplain of a home for the elderly in Lancaster, PA.

J

Lora Anne Jacob of Greensburg, PA, has been an Oblate of St. Benedict affiliated with St. Vincent Archabbey since September 22, 2013.

Louis Jacobs of Turnersville, NJ, has been an Oblate since November, 2008. He is very involved in his parish, through participation in two Bible studies and as a facilitator on a prayer line.

Br. Benedict Janecko, O.S.B., has been a professed monk of St. Vincent Archabbey since 1959. He has taught courses in Scripture for many years, with the psalms as his specialty. He is the author of the book *The Psalms: Heartbeat of Life and Worship*.

Deborah Johnston of Derry, PA, has been an Oblate of St. Benedict affiliated with St. Vincent Archabbey since 2009. She is also a retired educator and a musician.

K

Fr. Philip Kanfush, O.S.B., has been a professed monk of St. Vincent Archabbey since 1994. He currently serves as procurator of the Archabbey and teaches in the Education Department of St. Vincent College.

CONTRIBUTOR BIOGRAPHIES

MARY ANN KAUFMAN of Pittsburgh, PA, has been an Oblate of St. Benedict affiliated with St. Vincent Archabbey since 2010. Within the Oblate Program, she serves as the coordinator of the mentoring program, the prayer-partner program, and the *Directory*.

BR. DAVID KELLY, O.S.B., has been a professed monk of St. Vincent Archabbey since 1973. He currently serves as the Director of Libraries at St. Vincent and teaches canon law at St. Vincent Seminary.

CLAUDIA KNOWLTON of California, MD, has been an Oblate of St. Benedict affiliated with St. Vincent Archabbey since 2005.

L

BR. MATTHEW LAMBERT, O.S.B., has been a professed monk of St. Vincent Archabbey since 2010 and is currently a full-time student at St. Vincent Seminary. He also serves as a socius of the novices and as an assistant to the Director of Maintenance for the monastery.

PAULINE LANCIOTTI of Morgantown, WV, has been an Oblate of St. Benedict affiliated with St. Vincent Archabbey since April 17, 2013. She serves as the secretary of the group that meets at St. John University Parish in Morgantown.

CHERYL LAROSE of Charleston, SC, has been an Oblate of St. Benedict affiliated with St. Vincent Archabbey since 2012.

FREDERICK A. LAUX of Pendelton, IN, has been an Oblate of St. Benedict affiliated with St. Vincent Archabbey since May 23, 2013.

BR. HUGH LESTER, O.S.B., has been a professed monk of St. Vincent Archabbey since 1995. He currently serves as Director of Retreats, assistant to the Prior, and financial consultant to St. Vincent Seminary.

THE REV. DR. JEFF LOACH is Pastor of St. Paul's Presbyterian Church, Nobleton, Ontario, and an adjunct instructor in Spiritual Formation at Tyndale Seminary in Toronto. He has been an Oblate affiliated with St. Vincent Archabbey since 2011.

FR. KILLIAN LOCH, O.S.B., entered St. Vincent Archabbey in 2009 after serving 31 years as a priest in the Diocese of Scranton. Fr. Killian professed his first vows in 2010. He is currently Director of Campus Ministry for St. Vincent College.

M

BR. LAWRENCE MACHIA, O.S.B., has been a professed monk of St. Vincent Archabbey since July, 2013. He is currently a full-time student at St. Vincent Seminary and also works as an assistant in the Physics Department at St. Vincent College.

ALICIA MACK of Pittsburgh, PA, has been an Oblate novice affiliated with St. Vincent Archabbey since July 11, 2013. She resides in Upper St. Clair with her husband, Robert, and their three children. Alicia holds a doctorate in pharmacy and has a career with Allergan, Inc.

FR. EDWARD MAZICH, O.S.B., has been a professed monk of St. Vincent Archabbey since 1995. He currently serves as professor of theology at St. Vincent Seminary and directs the formation of solemnly professed monks who study in the seminary.

BR. CANICE MCMULLEN, O.S.B., has been a professed monk of St. Vincent Archabbey since 2011. In addition to full-time seminary studies, he has been working in the Archabbey's Vocation Office and also serves as assistant sacristan/master of ceremonies for the monastery.

SANDRA L. MONIER of Irwin, PA, has been an Oblate of St. Benedict affiliated with St. Vincent Archabbey since 2012. She is also an artist and currently serves as the DRE at St. Florian Parish in United, PA, and as a member of the auxiliary retreat staff at St. Paul of the Cross Passionist Retreat Center on the South Side of Pittsburgh.

BR. JOACHIM MORGAN, O.S.B., has been a professed monk of St. Vincent Archabbey since 2011. He is currently a full-time student at St. Vincent Seminary and also serves as the assistant Director of Oblates, as an assistant to the guest master, and as an assistant for the Retreat Program.

FR. PASCHAL A. MORLINO, O.S.B., has been a professed monk since 1960 and transferred his vows to St. Vincent Archabbey later in the 1960's. He is currently pastor of St. Benedict Parish in Baltimore, Maryland, and serves as Vice President of the North American Association of Benedictine

235

Oblate Directors. He is also the founder of Adelphoi Village in Latrobe, PA, and continues to serve on its board.

FR. NATHAN MUNSCH, O.S.B., has been a professed Benedictine monk since 1982 and a monk of Saint Vincent Archabbey for twenty years. He is an Assistant Professor of Theology in Saint Vincent College, an Instructor of Classical Languages, and a sacramental minister to St. Michael and St. Mary Parishes in Somerset County in the Diocese of Altoona-Johnstown.

N

ARCHABBOT DOUGLAS R. NOWICKI, O.S.B., has been the Archabbot of Saint Vincent Archabbey since January, 1991. He first professed vows in 1966 and was ordained a priest in 1972.

FR. JEFFREY S. NYARDY, O.S.B., has been a professed monk of St. Vincent Archabbey since 1986. He currently serves as the Master of Juniors of the monastery and as an assistant to the Archabbot.

P

FR. PAULO PANZA, O.S.B., is the prior of São Bento Monastery in Vinhedo, Brazil, and has been a professed monk of St. Vincent Archabbey since 1986.

FR. ALFRED PATTERSON, O.S.B., has been a professed monk of St. Vincent Archabbey since 1986. For two decades he served in various parishes, and after some time as full-time hospital chaplain for the Diocese of Greensburg, he is now serving as a hospital chaplain in St. Marys, PA, and as parochial vicar in two parishes in St. Marys.

CAROLYN VAN PELT has been an Oblate of St. Benedict affiliated with St. Vincent Archabbey since 2012. Her reflection on Chapter 72 of the *Rule* is an edited version of her blog, "Chapter 72 and the Holy Virgins."

JAMES PENNELL of Beaufort, SC, has been an Oblate of St. Benedict affiliated with St. Vincent Archabbey since April 21, 2013.

MARGARET PERHATS of McKeesport, PA, has been an Oblate of St. Benedict affiliated with St. Vincent Archabbey since 1991.

FR. NATHANAEL POLINSKI, O.S.B., has been a professed monk of St. Vincent Archabbey since 2006. He is currently a graduate student working for a licentiate in Scripture at the Catholic University of America in Washington, DC.

R

FR. DONALD RAILA, O.S.B., has been a professed monk of St. Vincent Archabbey since 1978. He has been the Director of Oblates since 1988 and an assistant organist since 1991.

EDWARD REZEK of Bethlehem, PA, has been an Oblate of St. Benedict affiliated with St. Vincent Archabbey since May 18, 2013.

LINDA ROCKEY of Latrobe, PA, has been an Oblate of St. Benedict affiliated with St. Vincent Archabbey since 1996 and is a psychologist.

CHRISTINE ROSSMILLER of Donegal, PA, has been an Oblate of St. Benedict affiliated with St. Vincent Archabbey since 2010. She is the mother of nine children and eight grandchildren and a retired shepherdess. Chris and her husband, John, live on their farm in Donegal.

S

FR. SEBASTIAN SAMAY, O.S.B., was a professed monk of St. Vincent Archabbey from 1955 until his sudden death on October 1, 2013. In his later years he was a professor emeritus of philosophy of St. Vincent College and continued to teach students in independent studies. He had also served as the Master of Novices for nearly 20 years.

PASTOR DOUGLAS SCHADER of Selinsgrove, PA, has been an Oblate of St. Benedict affiliated with St. Vincent Archabbey since 2011. He currently serves as pastor of Paradise United Church of Christ in Paradise, PA, and of Trinity Church of Christ in Milton, PA.

REV. SCOTT E. SCHUL has been an Oblate of St. Benedict affiliated with St. Vincent Archabbey since 2010 and serves as pastor of St. Matthew Lutheran Church in Martinsburg, PA, where he resides with his wife, daughter and son. Pastor Schul plays with four other pastors in a band that raises thousands of dollars for charity in the Blair County area, and he is a member of the Martinsburg Volunteer Fire Department.

CONTRIBUTOR BIOGRAPHIES

ANDREI SERGUEEV of Woodbridge, Ontario, Canada, has been an Oblate of St. Benedict affiliated with St. Vincent Archabbey since September 22, 2013. He works as a computer programmer in Toronto.

DONNA SUNSERI of Greensburg, PA, has been an Oblate of St. Benedict affiliated with St. Vincent Archabbey since 2005. She is a wife and a home-schooling mother of four children and also a graduate of St. Vincent College.

T

SR. MARIE TERESA TELLIER, C.H., has been an Oblate affiliated with St. Vincent Archabbey since 2011. She lives as a consecrated hermit of the Archdiocese of Baltimore at St. Gemma Hermitage in Cumberland, MD.

VINCENT THOMAS of Pittsburgh has been an Oblate of St. Benedict affiliated with St. Vincent Archabbey since 2012. He works in the financial-service industry and serves his parish, St. Therese in Munhall, in a number of ways, including membership on the parish financial council.

KATHRYNE THOMPSON of Richmond, VA, has been an Oblate of St. Benedict affiliated with St. Vincent Archabbey since May 18, 2013. At her home she stays busy taking care of three boys and painting, and she also does volunteer work.

FR. JOHN-MARY TOMPKINS, O.S.B., has been a professed monk of St. Vincent Archabbey since 1988. He currently serves as the Vice-Rector and Director of Pastoral Formation of St. Vincent Seminary.

THOMAS TROTTER of Riegelsville, PA, has been an Oblate of St. Benedict affiliated with St. Vincent Archabbey since 2012.

W

TERESA D. WARLOW of Liverpool, PA, has been an Oblate OF ST. Benedict affiliated with St. Vincent Archabbey since 2012.

JAMES "JAY" WELLS of Baltimore, MD, has been as Oblate of St. Benedict affiliated with St. Vincent Archabbey since August 15, 2010. He currently works as a certified public accountant and also serves as the secretary of the St. Walburga Deanery in Baltimore.

SUSAN WYKOFF of Lock Haven, PA, has been an Oblate of St. Benedict affiliated with St. Vincent Archabbey since July, 2010. Sue is an admissions counselor at Penn State University in State College, PA, and attends Holy Spirit Parish in Lock Haven.

Z

DIANE ZELENAK of Greensburg, PA, has been an Oblate novice of St. Benedict affiliated with St. Vincent Archabbey since March 21, 2013. A graduate of Seton Hill College, she has a B.A. in mathematics and works for the Commonwealth of Pennsylvania as a disability claims adjudicator. Diane also belongs to Saint Vincent Basilica Parish.

CONTRIBUTOR BIOGRAPHIES

BR. MARTINHO ZEVALLOS, O.S.B., has been a professed monk of São Bento Priory in Vinhedo, Brazil, a dependency of St. Vincent Archabbey, since 2011.

Reading Schedule

Dates	Chapter: Lines
Jan 1-May 2-Sep 1	Prol: 1-7
Jan 2-May 3-Sep 2	Prol: 8-13
Jan 3-May 4-Sep 3	Prol: 14-21
Jan 4-May 5-Sep 4	Prol: 22-34
Jan 5-May 6-Sep 5	Prol: 35-38
Jan 6-May 7-Sep 6	Prol: 39-44
Jan 7-May 8-Sep 7	Prol: 45-50
Jan 8-May 9-Sep 8	1:1-13
Jan 9-May 10-Sep 9	2:1-5
Jan 10-May 11-Sep10	2:6-10
Jan 11-May 12-Sep 11	2:11-15
Jan 12-May 13-Sep 12	2:16-22
Jan 13-May 14-Sep 13	2:23-29
Jan 14-May 15-Sep 14	2:30-36
Jan 15-May 16-Sep 15	2:37-40
Jan 16-May 17-Sep 16	3:1-6
Jan 17-May 18-Sep 17	3:7-13
Jan 18-May 19-Sep 18	4:1-19
Jan 19-May 20-Sep 19	4:20-43
Jan 20-May 21-Sep 20	4:44-61
Jan 21-May 22-Sep 21	4:62-78
Jan 22-May 23-Sep 22	5:1-13
Jan 23-May 24-Sep 23	5:14-19
Jan 24-May 25-Sep 24	6:1-8
Jan 25-May 26-Sep 25	7:1-9
Jan 26-May 27-Sep 26	7:10-13
Jan 27-May 28-Sep 27	7:14-18
Jan 28-May 29-Sep 28	7:19-22
Jan 29-May 30-Sep 29	7:23-30
Jan 30-May 31-Sep 30	7:31-33
Jan 31-Jun 1-Oct 1	7:34
Feb 1-Jun 2-Oct 2	7:35-43
Feb 2-Jun 3-Oct 3	7:44-48

THE RULE IN BITS AND PIECES

Dates	Chapter: Lines
Feb 3-Jun 4-Oct 4	7:49-50
Feb 4-Jun 5-Oct 5	7:51-54
Feb 5-Jun 6-Oct 6	7:55
Feb 6-Jun 7-Oct 7	7:56-58
Feb 7-Jun 8-Oct 8	7:59
Feb 8 -Jun 9-Oct 9	7:60-61
Feb 9-Jun 10-Oct 10	7:62-70
Feb 10-Jun 11-Oct 11	8:1-4
Feb 11-Jun 12-Oct 12	9:1-11
Feb 12-Jun 13-Oct 13	10:1-3
Feb 13-Jun 14-Oct 14	11:1-13
Feb 14-Jun 15-Oct 15	12:1-4
Feb 15-Jun 16-Oct 16	13:1-11
Feb 16-Jun 17-Oct 17	13:12-14
Feb 17-Jun 18-Oct 18	14:1-2
Feb 18-Jun 19-Oct 19	15:1-4
Feb 19-Jun 20-Oct 20	16:1-5
Feb 20-Jun 21-Oct 21	17:1-10
Feb 21-Jun 22-Oct 22	18:1-6
Feb 22-Jun 23-Oct 23	18:7-11
Feb 23-Jun 24-Oct 24	18:12-19
Feb 23 (24*)-Jun 25-Oct 25	18:20-25
Feb 24 (25*)-Jun 26-Oct 26	19:1-7
Feb 25 (26*)-Jun 27-Oct 27	20:1-5
Feb 26 (27*)-Jun 28-Oct 28	21:1-7
Feb 27 (28*)-Jun 29-Oct 29	22:1-8
Feb 28 (29*)-Jun 30-Oct 30	23:1-5
Mar 1-Jul 1-Oct 31	24:1-7
Mar 2-Jul 2-Nov 1	25:1-6
Mar 3-Jul 3-Nov 2	26:1-2
Mar 4-Jul 4-Nov 3	27:1-9
Mar 5-Jul 5-Nov 4	28:1-8
Mar 6-Jul 6-Nov 5	29:1-3
Mar 7-Jul 7-Nov 6	30:1-3
Mar 8-Jul 8-Nov 7	31:1-12

* Leap years. Read both Feb 23 readings in non leap years.

READING SCHEDULE

Dates	Chapter: Lines
Mar 9-Jul 9-Nov 8	31:13-19
Mar 10-Jul 10-Nov 9	32:1-5
Mar 11-Jul 11-Nov 10	33:1-8
Mar 12-Jul 12-Nov 11	34:1-7
Mar 13-Jul 13-Nov 12	35:1-11
Mar 14-Jul 14-Nov 13	35:12-18
Mar 15-Jul 15-Nov 14	36:1-10
Mar 16-Jul 16-Nov 15	37:1-3
Mar 17-Jul 17-Nov 16	38:1-12
Mar 18-Jul 18-Nov 17	39:1-11
Mar 19-Jul 19-Nov 18	40:1-9
Mar 20-Jul 20-Nov 19	41:1-9
Mar 21-Jul 21-Nov 20	42:1-11
Mar 22-Jul 22-Nov 21	43:1-9
Mar 23-Jul 23-Nov 22	43:10-19
Mar 24-Jul 24-Nov 23	44:1-10
Mar 25-Jul 25-Nov 24	45:1-3
Mar 26-Jul 26-Nov 25	46:1-6
Mar 27-Jul 27-Nov 26	47:1-4
Mar 28-Jul 28-Nov 27	48:1-9
Mar 29-Jul 29-Nov 28	48:10-21
Mar 30-Jul 30-Nov 29	48:22-25
Mar 31-Jul 31-Nov 30	49:1-10
Apr 1-Aug 1-Dec 1	50:1-4
Apr 2-Aug 2-Dec 2	51:1-3
Apr 3-Aug 3-Dec 3	52:1-5
Apr 4-Aug 4-Dec 4	53:1-14
Apr 5-Aug 5-Dec 5	53:15-24
Apr 6-Aug 6-Dec 6	54:1-5
Apr 7-Aug 7-Dec 7	55:1-14
Apr 8-Aug 8-Dec 8	55:15-22
Apr 9-Aug 9-Dec 9	56:1-3
Apr 10-Aug 10-Dec 10	57:1-9
Apr 11-Aug11-Dec 11	58:1-16
Apr 12-Aug 12-Dec 12	58:17-29
Apr 13-Aug 13-Dec 13	59:1-8
Apr 14-Aug 14-Dec 14	60:1-9

THE RULE IN BITS AND PIECES

Dates	Chapter: Lines
Apr 15-Aug 15-Dec 15	61:1-7
Apr 16-Aug 16-Dec 16	61:8-14
Apr 17-Aug 17-Dec 17	62:1-11
Apr 18-Aug 18-Dec 18	63:1-9
Apr 19-Aug 19-Dec 19	63:10-19
Apr 20-Aug 20-Dec 20	64:1-6
Apr 21-Aug 21-Dec 21	64:7-22
Apr 22-Aug 22-Dec 22	65:1-10
Apr 23-Aug 23-Dec 23	65:11-22
Apr 24-Aug 24-Dec 24	66:1-8
Apr 25-Aug 25-Dec 25	67:1-7
Apr 26-Aug 26-Dec 26	68:1-5
Apr 27-Aug 27-Dec 27	69:1-4
Apr 28-Aug 28-Dec 28	70:1-7
Apr 29-Aug 29-Dec 29	71:1-9
Apr 30-Aug 30-Dec 30	72:1-12
May 1-Aug 31-Dec 31	73:1-9

Other Titles

PUBLISHED BY

SACRED WINDS PRESS

Available World-Wide and at www.sacredwindspress.com.

Prayer, Study, and Work: Renewing the Benedictine Ideal. Daniel J. Heisey succinctly explores what Benedictines and other Christians immersed in a modern suburban culture can learn from the vision of monastic saints such as Benedict and Basil. Using the documents of the Second Vatican Council and other texts, Heisey meditates upon ways to pursue a path of renewal through the Benedictine ideals of prayer, study, and work. Paperback. 72 pages.

Yet All Shall Be Well. Written over the course of ten years, and spanning America, England, and continental Europe, twenty-five poems make up Yet All Shall Be Well. Using three American and English poetic voices, Daniel J. Heisey's poems touch on the spiritual found in the ordinary. The daily, spiritual scenes of ordinary men and women are sketched for the reader to view and contemplate. Paperback. 46 pages.

Lessons from Saint Benedict. Part of a collection written over twenty years, Lessons from Saint Benedict contains 26 letters written by Donald Raila, O.S.B., a Benedictine monk of Saint Vincent Archabbey. Using the 1500 year old Rule of Benedict and Benedictine spirituality as his foundation, Father Donald offers words of spiritual encouragement and guidance for persevering through the journey of daily life. With the Gospel and Rule of Benedict as guides, Raila says, we can learn to see God's graces in every dimension of our lives, even the most seemingly mundane. Father Donald provides both serious and light-hearted examples from his own life to demonstrate how we can renew and strengthen our spirituality through the daily grind, and perhaps even find joy in the process. Paperback. 202 pages.

The Study Guide to Lessons from Saint Benedict. An excellent resource for groups and individuals who would like to further their studies and enhance spiritual growth through Father Donald Raila's book Lessons from Saint Benedict. Each chapter includes three study questions and three suggested activities designed to encourage group discussions and individual reflections. Paperback. 68 pages.

Flowers in the Desert. The bible is, above all other things, a record of God's love for the human race. In its words and through its stories God reveals himself and calls those who hear the word into communion with him. When we first approach the bible, however, we encounter a variety of literary styles—histories, poetry, sagas, moral advice and visionary productions. There is often a problem of discerning the simple theme of call-and-response in all these styles, or of finding a connection in the bible to our 20th century existence. This book opens the door to the deep message the bible conveys to individual Christians today. Putting aside for a moment questions of doctrine or historical interpretation, it concentrates on the spiritual teaching of the Old and New Testaments. It begins with God's call to humanity and to each of us individually. Then it considers the human adventure of our journey through life. Finally it looks at our ultimate homecoming to the Father. The many references to biblical passages and daily life make this an invaluable book for those who want to know about the bible—but even more, who want to live it. By Demetrius Dumm. eBook.

So We Do Not Lose Heart. This book contains 83 short reflections on passages of scripture which address, from various perspectives, the perennial human problem of mortality. A prominent theme in these reflections is, therefore, an invitation to trust the goodness of God in situations where we experience loss of control and the consequent need to rely on a higher power for love and support. These reflections also remind us that reliance on the goodness of God need not be a desperate last resort but can in fact be a joyful discovery that will illuminate the whole landscape of our lives. By Demetrius Dumm. eBook.

The Psalms. This book points believers to this ageless prayer book of life. Examining the major themes of the Psalms, the author tries to rescue the impassioned cry of the psalmist from superficial piety and disuse. Brother Benedict Janecko, O.S.B., shows that one finds the heart of religious experience in ordinary living, whether we are "on a high," "in the pits," or somewhere in between. The reader of this small book will recognize his or her own struggle to trust, to forgive, to repent, to wonder, to endure, to cope, to find meaning, to get along, to express oneself — and in doing so, will know the truest religious experience: God living and reigning within one's own life. eBook.

Saint Vincent Seminary from Its Origins to the Present. Saint Vincent Seminary is the oldest major seminary in the United States operated by Benedictine monks. Canonically established in 1855 by Pope Pius IX, the Seminary's roots lie much farther back in time. With the new millennium, the Seminary enters its third century: during that time it has given the Church more than forty bishops and abbots, both in America and in Europe. Also among its alumni are musicians and historians, labor priests and biblical scholars. This history traces the growth of the Seminary from its origins in Bavaria to its activities today, while keeping in view the wider field of Christendom. By Daniel J. Heisey. eBook.